THE
EVERYDAY
GUIDE TO...
PROPHECY

THE EVERYDAY GUIDE TO...

PROPHECY

Carol Smith

HUMBLECREEK
INSPIRATION FOR LIFE

© 2005 by Barbour Publishing, Inc.

Produced with the assistance of The Livingstone Corporation
(www.Livingstonecorp.com).
Project staff includes Christopher Hudson, Don Jones, Carol Smith,
and Mary Horner Collins.

ISBN 1-59310-726-9

All scripture quotations, unless otherwise noted, are taken from the King James
Version of the Bible.

Published by Humble Creek, P.O. Box 719, Uhrichsville, Ohio 44683

Printed in the United States of America.
5 4 3 2 1

Contents

Introduction

Many people consider studying the end times as a curious and eccentric pursuit. Perhaps they have become disillusioned by the precise predictions of "prophecy experts" and the constantly revised interpretations that fit every new political crisis. But, the fact is, we can't ignore what the Bible says about the end of the world. After all, our hope and vision for the future shape our actions.

In the absence of a specific timetable, how should we live in the face of Christ's imminent return? As you might expect, the Bible has plenty to say on the subject. And as you may expect, people have many different views on the subject. Through these daily readings you will look at the end times through several different prisms, along with the Scriptures used to support them.

Christians throughout history have generally approached the book of Revelation from four different viewpoints. Each view has its strengths. None has been able to argue the others out of existence. We must be careful, though. Each view can also be misused. We will never know the exact time or date of Jesus' return (Mark 13:32–33). But God does expect us to be ready for his return.

Read the verses. Read the thoughts. Ask yourself the questions. Then, determine how you can best live prepared to be accountable before God through his grace.

TABLE: TYPES OF END-TIMES INTERPRETATIONS

View	Explanation	Reasoning
Futurist View (It's all in the future.)	Only the letters to the churches (Revelation 1–3) are directed to John's contemporaries. The rest of the book describes the end of history.	Every generation can find reason to accept the possibility of Christ's imminent return, while resisting the temptation to set dates for it.
Historicist View (It happened in history.)	Revelation is a foretelling of all of history, from John's day until the end of time.	Every generation should note how Revelation accurately portrays the battle between good and evil throughout world history.
Preterist View (It happened in the first century.)	John was writing a highly figurative message of encouragement to fellow believers facing terrible persecution under the Roman Empire.	Readers throughout the centuries have gained comfort from evidence of God's power and judgment no matter what their situation. At the same time, we may conclude that John's writing, like other biblical prophecies, contains both immediate and long-term references.
Symbolic View (It's all symbolic.)	John was writing a timeless figurative description of the ebb and flow of evil in the world.	Today's readers can learn lessons from the past, readying themselves for the future and focusing their attention on Jesus Christ today.

Day 1

But now is Christ risen from the dead, and become the firstfruits
of them that slept. For since by man came death, by man came
also the resurrection of the dead. For as in Adam all die, even so in
Christ shall all be made alive. But every man in his own order:
Christ the firstfruits; afterward they that are Christ's at his coming.
Then cometh the end, when he shall have delivered up the kingdom
to God, even the Father; when he shall have put down all rule and
all authority and power. For he must reign, till he hath put all enemies
under his feet. The last enemy that shall be destroyed is death.

1 Corinthians 15:20–26

Who shall lay any thing to the charge of God's elect?
It is God that justifieth. Who is he that condemneth?
It is Christ that died, yea rather, that is risen again,
who is even at the right hand of God,
who also maketh intercession for us.

Romans 8:33–34

And when all things shall be subdued unto him,
then shall the Son also himself be subject unto him that put
all things under him, that God may be all in all.

1 Corinthians 15:28

THE BIG PICTURE

While there is diversity among believers regarding the precise order of events in the end times, we all agree on the "big picture." Jesus changed the destiny of human history. Though his promised future reign is not yet fully here, his life, death, and resurrection are its guarantee. Jesus' resurrection promises his followers a future life (after death) where evil no longer exists (1 Corinthians 15:20–26).

After Jesus has defeated all of his enemies, he will return as the final Judge. He will hold all people accountable for their actions. On that day, Jesus will finally answer the cries for justice (Revelation 6:9). Believers know that when we appear before the final Judge, we won't have to rely on our own works. Our Lord and Savior will cover our sins and accept us (Romans 8:33–34). After establishing his kingdom, Christ will control everything forevermore (1 Corinthians 15:28).

Need to Know

- Jesus was called the *firstfruits*. The firstfruits were the firstborn of any family or herd, or the first parts of any crop. The firstfruits were seen as holy, belonging only to God. Jesus was the first of the resurrected souls.
- God claims us righteous through our faith in Christ. This is what is referred to as *justification*.

Think About It

- Do you fear God's judgment, or do you feel justified in his eyes because of his grace?
- When you think of being accountable to God, what would you most like to change about your life?

Day 2

These all died in faith, not having received the promises,
but having seen them afar off, and were persuaded of them,
and embraced them, and confessed that they were strangers
and pilgrims on the earth.
HEBREWS 11:13

But the day of the Lord will come as a thief in the night;
in the which the heavens shall pass away with a great noise,
and the elements shall melt with fervent heat, the earth also
and the works that are therein shall be burned up. Seeing then
that all these things shall be dissolved, what manner of persons
ought ye to be in all holy conversation and godliness?
2 PETER 3:10–11

Go ye therefore, and teach all nations, baptizing them in the name
of the Father, and of the Son, and of the Holy Ghost:
Teaching them to observe all things whatsoever
I have commanded you: and, lo, I am with you alway,
even unto the end of the world. Amen.
MATTHEW 28:19–20

And all things are of God, who hath reconciled us to himself
by Jesus Christ, and hath given to us the ministry of reconciliation;
To wit, that God was in Christ, reconciling the world unto himself,
not imputing their trespasses unto them; and hath committed unto us the
word of reconciliation. Now then we are ambassadors for Christ,
as though God did beseech you by us: we pray you in Christ's stead,
be ye reconciled to God. For he hath made him to be sin for us, who
knew no sin; that we might be made the righteousness of God in him.
2 CORINTHIANS 5:18–21

Living Near the End

Believers should eagerly seek Christ's return, not the world's applause (Hebrews 11:13). Jesus outlined the signs of the last days precisely so that we will be watchful. Does your life exemplify Christ's love for the lost (2 Peter 3:10–11)? Are you spreading the Good News (Matthew 28:19–20)?

In this world we will continue to face struggles. Yet the fact that Christ has assured our future with him adds a unique dimension to the Christian life. Our future is already guaranteed—eternity with God. Because of that fact, we can reflect Jesus' self-sacrificial love without fear. We can spend our lives for Jesus' sake (2 Corinthians 5:18–21).

Christ is the basis for our hope in the future. As Christians, we eagerly look forward to Christ's future reign and seek to reflect his sacrificial love in our world today.

Need to Know
- *Hebrews 11* is sometimes called the "Hall of Faith." People such as Abraham, Sarah, Moses, David, and Samuel all looked toward Christ's coming, even though it didn't happen in their lifetime.
- *Reconciliation* is actually an accounting term. It means to make both sides equal. When we take part in the ministry of reconciliation, we communicate God's grace to others who, like us, don't deserve it. Through that grace, God makes us righteous.

Think About It
- In what ways does your life reflect Christ?
- To whom around you would you like to spread the gospel of Jesus?

DAY 3

And Jesus answered and said unto them,
Take heed that no man deceive you.
For many shall come in my name, saying, I am Christ;
and shall deceive many. And ye shall hear of wars and rumours of wars:
see that ye be not troubled: for all these things must come to pass,
but the end is not yet. For nation shall rise against nation,
and kingdom against kingdom: and there shall be famines,
and pestilences, and earthquakes, in divers places.
All these are the beginning of sorrows. . . .
Immediately after the tribulation of those days
shall the sun be darkened,
and the moon shall not give her light,
and the stars shall fall from heaven,
and the powers of the heavens shall be shaken.
MATTHEW 24:4–8, 29

And when ye shall hear of wars and rumours of wars,
be ye not troubled: for such things must needs be;
but the end shall not be yet. . . .
But of that day and that hour knoweth no man,
no, not the angels which are in heaven, neither the Son,
but the Father. . . . But take ye heed: behold,
I have foretold you all things.
MARK 13:7, 32, 23

And there shall be signs in the sun, and in the moon,
and in the stars; and upon the earth distress of nations,
with perplexity; the sea and the waves roaring.
LUKE 21:25

Signs of the Times

False Christs, wars, and famines—these are the signs that characterize our fallen world (Matthew 24:4–8). We shouldn't assume the end of the world is near when false messiahs, wars, and famines appear. In fact, the end may still be far off (Mark 13:7). However, these terrifying events serve as reminders to us that we cannot save ourselves. Only Christ can defeat the evil that is rampant in this world.

God's coming judgment will also be preceded by falling stars, eclipses, earthquakes, and other catastrophes (Matthew 24:29; Luke 21:25). These natural catastrophes will constitute God's final call to repentance. National leaders will be confused. People will faint in horror.

Scripture doesn't give us these signs so we can calculate the year and date when the world will end. Jesus told his disciples no one knows the date or hour (Mark 13:32). Instead, he simply warned them, "Be on your guard!" (Mark 13:23).

Need to Know

- False Christs or antichrists have appeared since the first century. John mentioned in his letters that many antichrists had already appeared. These were people who denied that Jesus was the Son of God (1 John 2:18–22).
- Jesus gives two parables in Matthew 25 regarding the judgment of people's lives. One is based on the story of servants who have been left in charge of their master's money. The other is a story about sheep and goats. In both, people face a reckoning for the way they have "spent" their lives.

Think About It

- What are some "signs" that you see around you of the natural catastrophes described in today's Scripture reading?
- What do you see as the benefits or distractions of trying to pin down the time of Christ's return?

TABLE: Signs of the Times

Sign	Reference
• People living as if God didn't exist	Genesis 6:5; Luke 17:26–27
• Explosion of knowledge and freedom of travel	Daniel 12:4
• Wars and rumors of wars	Mark 13:7
• Widespread acceptance of immoral behavior	Luke 17:26–30; 2 Peter 2:5–8
• Vacuum in world leadership	Psalm 2:1–3; Revelation 13:4–9
• Increased demonic activity	1 Timothy 4:1–3
• Widespread abandonment of the Christian faith	1 Timothy 4:1; 2 Timothy 4:3–4
• Evidence of breakdown in families	2 Timothy 3:1–3
• Spirit of selfishness and materialism	2 Timothy 3:1–2
• General disrespect for others	2 Timothy 3:2–4
• Human leader declares himself to be god	2 Thessalonians 2:3–4
• People ridiculing God's Word	2 Peter 3:2–4; Jude 17–18
• Significant shifts in political power and influence	Revelation 13:3–7

Day 4

When ye therefore shall see the abomination of desolation,
spoken of by Daniel the prophet, stand in the holy place,
(whoso readeth, let him understand:)
Then let them which be in Judaea flee into the mountains:
Let him which is on the housetop not come down to take
any thing out of his house: Neither let him which is in the field
return back to take his clothes. And woe unto them that are with child,
and to them that give suck in those days! But pray ye that your flight
be not in the winter, neither on the sabbath day: For then shall be great
tribulation, such as was not since the beginning of the world to this time,
no, nor ever shall be. . . . And then shall appear the sign of the Son of
man in heaven: and then shall all the tribes of the earth mourn,
and they shall see the Son of man coming in the clouds
of heaven with power and great glory.
MATTHEW 24:15–21, 30

Let no man deceive you by any means: for that day shall not come,
except there come a falling away first, and that man of sin be revealed,
the son of perdition; Who opposeth and exalteth himself above
all that is called God, or that is worshipped; so that he as God
sitteth in the temple of God, shewing himself that he is God.
Remember ye not, that, when I was yet with you, I told you these things?
And now ye know what withholdeth that he might be revealed in his
time. For the mystery of iniquity doth already work: only he who now
letteth will let, until he be taken out of the way. And then shall that
Wicked be revealed, whom the Lord shall consume with the spirit
of his mouth, and shall destroy with the brightness of his coming.
2 THESSALONIANS 2:3–8

THE ANTICHRIST

Two decisive signs will indicate the end of the world is near. First, the antichrist will defile the temple ("the abomination of desolation"). After that, a period of wickedness and intense persecution of God's people—the Great Tribulation—will follow (see Matthew 24:15–18). Postmillennialists believe that Christ's prophecy of the defilement of the temple was already fulfilled when Jerusalem was destroyed by the Romans in A.D. 70 (Matthew 24:15). However, most Christians believe that this event merely foreshadowed the horrific events that will occur at the end times. In the last days the antichrist will desecrate the temple with a disgusting and blasphemous ritual and afterwards lead a ferocious campaign against God's people. This time will be a period of great suffering (Matthew 24:19–21). His reign of terror will only be stopped by Christ, who will return in glory (Matthew 24:30). Paul also predicted that a "man of sin. . .the son of perdition" would appear right before Jesus' second coming (2 Thessalonians 2:3–8).

Need to Know
- From the earliest Old Testament history of the Jewish nation, God always required purity of worship from his people. This highlights the significance of the defilement of the temple, which is an act of abandoning the most sacred requirement—to worship God alone.
- The *man of sin* that Paul wrote about was also referred to as the "son of perdition" and the "man doomed to destruction." Paul noted that this person would eventually be overthrown by Jesus, but before that he would work against the cause of Christ.

Think About It
- What concerns you the most when you think about a world power—bent on working against the cause of Christ—rising in the end times?
- What efforts do you see in your world today that might represent the work of a kind of antiChrist?

DAY 5

Then shall they deliver you up to be afflicted, and shall kill you:
and ye shall be hated of all nations for my name's sake.
And then shall many be offended, and shall betray one another,
and shall hate one another. And many false prophets shall rise,
and shall deceive many. And because iniquity shall abound,
the love of many shall wax cold. But he that shall endure unto the end,
the same shall be saved. . . . For there shall arise false Christs,
and false prophets, and shall shew great signs and wonders;
insomuch that, if it were possible, they shall deceive the very elect. . . .
But as the days of Noe were, so shall also the coming of
the Son of man be. For as in the days that were before the flood
they were eating and drinking, marrying and giving in marriage,
until the day that Noe entered into the ark,
And knew not until the flood came, and took them all away;
so shall also the coming of the Son of man be.
MATTHEW 24:9–13, 24, 37–39

Even him, whose coming is after the working of Satan
with all power and signs and lying wonders,
And with all deceivableness of unrighteousness in them that perish;
because they received not the love of the truth, that they might be saved.
And for this cause God shall send them strong delusion,
that they should believe a lie:
That they all might be damned who believed not the truth,
but had pleasure in unrighteousness.
2 THESSALONIANS 2:9–12

This know also, that in the last days perilous times shall come.
For men shall be lovers of their own selves,
covetous, boasters, proud, blasphemers,
disobedient to parents, unthankful, unholy,
Without natural affection, trucebreakers, false accusers,
incontinent, fierce, despisers of those that are good,
Traitors, heady, high-minded, lovers of pleasures
more than lovers of God; Having a form of godliness,
but denying the power thereof: from such turn away.
2 TIMOTHY 3:1–5

Rampant Evil

Wickedness will become rampant in the last days (Matthew 24:37–39). Violence, hedonism, and arrogance will lead to a breakdown of the social order (2 Timothy 3:1–5). Jesus warned his followers that they will be hated by all nations and even betrayed by their families (Matthew 24:9–10).

In the last days, many who claim to be God's people will lose their faith (Matthew 24:11–12, 24). Due to the increasing wickedness, "the love of many shall wax cold" (Matthew 24:12). Many will be deceived by false teachers who will lead them away from God (2 Thessalonians 2:9–12; 1 John 2:22; 4:2–3; 2 John 1:7). Jesus described all these signs to his disciples so that his true followers would remain faithful in spite of these troubles and catastrophes. Only the person "that shall endure unto the end shall be saved" (Matthew 24:13).

Need to Know
- Jesus compared the last days to the days when Noah lived. In the book of Genesis we are told that Noah found grace in God's eyes. In terms of the rest of humanity though, God was grieved, almost repentant of his creation (Genesis 6:6–7).
- These passages reveal the dark side of humanity that will be so evident as time grows short. As we endure these times, we should ask God to develop the fruits of the Holy Spirit in us: love, joy, peace, long-suffering, gentleness, goodness, faith, meekness, and temperance (Galatians 5:22–23).

Think About It
- How would you outline the false teachings you hear around you?
- How would you describe someone who has "lost his faith"?

Day 6

But when they persecute you in this city,
flee ye into another: for verily I say unto you,
Ye shall not have gone over the cities of Israel,
till the Son of man be come.
MATTHEW 10:23

And this gospel of the kingdom shall be preached in
all the world for a witness unto all nations;
and then shall the end come.
MATTHEW 24:14

I say then, Hath God cast away his people? God forbid.
For I also am an Israelite, of the seed of Abraham,
of the tribe of Benjamin. . . . What then?
Israel hath not obtained that which he seeketh for;
but the election hath obtained it, and the rest were blinded
(According as it is written, God hath given them the spirit of slumber,
eyes that they should not see, and ears that they should not hear;)
unto this day. And David saith, Let their table be made a snare,
and a trap, and a stumbling block, and a recompence unto them:
Let their eyes be darkened, that they may not see,
and bow down their back alway. I say then,
Have they stumbled that they should fall?
God forbid: but rather through their fall salvation is come
unto the Gentiles, for to provoke them to jealousy.
Now if the fall of them be the riches of the world,
and the diminishing of them the riches of the Gentiles;
how much more their fulness?
ROMANS 11:1, 7–12

Good News for All

Not all the signs of the end times are terrifying and horrific. Jesus also told his disciples that the Good News of Christ would reach all nations before he returned (Matthew 24:14; Mark 13:10).

Jesus also predicted that the Good News will be preached to all Israel before he returns (Matthew 10:23). Jesus anticipated Israel's future conversion, thus fulfilling many Old Testament prophecies (for example, Ezekiel 36:22–32). Paul explained that God has allowed the non-Jews to come to Christ because of the Jews' rejection of him. Later, the Jews will also be saved (Romans 11:1, 11–12, 25–26). When Christ returns, Jew and Christian will finally be reconciled as part of the same olive tree (Romans 11:17–24). Many amillennialists reject this last sign. They see the church as fulfilling these promises, because they believe it is the true Israel.

Need to Know
- Christianity grew out of Judaism, which was both a faith and a lineage of people based on God's promise to Abraham to raise a nation from his descendants and to give them a land of their own (Genesis 17:5–8). Abraham's descendants, the Jews, have struggled throughout history to maintain their land and their very existence. As Christianity developed into a movement on its own, embracing all humanity, it could have seemed to the Jews that their distinctive as God's people was being watered down.

Think About It
- Do you believe the gospel has been preached throughout the world?
- What do you see as your responsibility on a daily basis in spreading that gospel to all people?

DAY 7

Ye men of Galilee, why stand ye gazing up into heaven?
this same Jesus, which is taken up from you into heaven,
shall so come in like manner as ye have seen him go into heaven.

ACTS 1:11

And I saw heaven opened, and behold a white horse;
and he that sat upon him was called Faithful and True,
and in righteousness he doth judge and make war.
His eyes were as a flame of fire, and on his head were many crowns;
and he had a name written, that no man knew, but he himself.
And he was clothed with a vesture dipped in blood:
and his name is called The Word of God.
And the armies which were in heaven followed him
upon white horses, clothed in fine linen, white and clean.
And out of his mouth goeth a sharp sword,
that with it he should smite the nations: and
he shall rule them with a rod of iron: and he treadeth the
winepress of the fierceness and wrath of Almighty God.
And he hath on his vesture and on his thigh a name written,
KING OF KINGS, AND LORD OF LORDS.

REVELATION 19:11–16

Various Views on How the World Will End

How will this world end? When will it happen? Will there be any warning signs when it's about to occur? These and many other questions have plagued diligent students of the book of Revelation. Revelation does give us some clues. It describes bloody wars, horrendous hailstorms, and ghastly plagues. In the middle of this chaos, Jesus, the King of kings, returns to the earth to save his people and pronounce judgment on his enemies (Revelation 16:17–21; 19:11–18). There's no question that Jesus will one day return to the earth (Acts 1:11). All Christians believe this. But exactly how Jesus will return and the order of events before his coming has been debated for centuries. There are four main views about how the world will end—dispensational premillennialism, historic premillennialism, postmillennialism, and amillennialism. Each of these views differs in the order of events surrounding Christ's return and even the existence of events. Most differ in terms of when Christ will return in light of the thousand-year (millennial) reign, and whether that reign is a literal one.

Need to Know
- Revelation 20:1–6 is the primary text for the *Millennium,* the thousand-year reign of Christ. Some view this reign in a literal sense, one that will be experienced on earth. Others view it as a symbolic of Christ's eternal rule.
- While there are many different views on the end of the world, it will include both the gathering of believers and the reckoning of all people before God's judgment.

Think About It
- What are you most curious about in regards to the timing of the events surrounding Christ's return?
- How do you think Christians should function together in light of their many different understandings about the end of the world?

TABLE: VIEWS ON THE EVENTS OF THE LAST DAYS

Event	Dispensational Premillennialism	Historic Premillennialism	Amillennialism	Postmillennialism
Rapture	The church is raptured prior to the Tribulation and taken to heaven to be with Christ.	The Rapture is part of the Second Coming—when believers join Christ in the air to descend to earth with him.	The Rapture is part of the Second Coming—when believers join Christ in the air to descend to earth with him.	The Rapture is part of the Second Coming— when believers join Christ in the air to descend to earth with him.
Israel and the church	Israel and the church have entirely different destinies in the end times.	The church is the "spiritual Israel," fulfilling the Old Testament prophecies concerning Israel, though some are reserved for Israel itself.	The church is the "spiritual Israel," fulfilling the Old Testament prophecies regarding Israel.	The church is the "spiritual Israel," fulfilling the Old Testament prophecies concerning Israel.
Antichrist	The antichrist is a person who will appear during the end times to personify satanic power. He will make a treaty with Israel and then persecute that nation.	The antichrist is a person who will appear during the end times to personify satanic power.	The antichrist represents satanic power throughout this age. Perhaps a person, personifying satanic power at the end of our age, will appear.	The antichrist represents satanic power throughout the church age. Most biblical references to the antichrist have already been fulfilled.
Tribulation	The church is raptured to heaven before the Tribulation. Israel is converted through the Tribulation.	The church goes through the Tribulation.	The church goes through the Tribulation, which is a final outbreak of evil at the end of this age.	The Tribulation is this present age. Evil lessens towards the end of this age.

Event	Dispensational Premillennialism	Historic Premillennialism	Amillennialism	Postmillennialism
Armageddon	Armageddon is the final rebellion against God before Christ establishes the Millennium. The church is absent during this period.	Armageddon is the final rebellion against God before Christ establishes the Millennium. The church is present during this period.	Armageddon is the final rebellion against God at the end of this age. The church is present during this period.	Armageddon is a picture of the heavenly Christ leading the church to victory over all its enemies through the power of the Good News.
Second Coming	The Second Coming will occur in two phrases. First, the church will be raptured. Seven years later, Christ will return to earth to establish the Millennium.	Jesus' Second Coming will establish the Millennium.	Jesus' Second Coming will establish the new heaven and new earth.	Jesus' Second Coming after the Millennium will establish the new heaven and new earth.
Resurrection	The resurrection will occur in three phases: (1) the resurrection of dead believers at the Rapture, (2) the resurrection of Old Testament saints and tribulation martyrs at Jesus' Second Coming, and (3) the resurrection of the remaining dead at the end of the Millennium.	The resurrection will occur in two phases: (1) the resurrection of all dead believers at Jesus' Second Coming, and (2) the resurrection of the remaining dead at the end of the Millennium.	One general resurrection of believing and unbelieving dead will occur at the Second Coming.	One general resurrection of believing and unbelieving dead will occur at the Second Coming.

Event	Dispensational Premillennialism	Historic Premillennialism	Amillennialism	Postmillennialism
Judgment	Judgment will occur in three phases. (1) At the Rapture, believers' works will be judged. (2) At the Second Coming, Gentiles and living Jews will be judged so that only believers enter the Millennium. Resurrected Old Testament saints and tribulation martyrs with positions in the Millennium will be judged. (3) At the end of the Millennium, unbelievers will face the large, white throne judgment.	Judgment will occur in two phases. (1) At the Second Coming, believers' works will be judged. (2) At the end of the Millennium, everyone will face the final judgment.	At the Second Coming, all people will be judged.	At the Second Coming, occurring at the end of the Millennium, there will be one judgment of all people.
Millennium	The Millennium is a thousand-year period that fulfills Old Testament promises for the nation of Israel. Jesus reigns literally in Jerusalem. The curse is removed from the earth. The church is in heaven.	Jesus reigns visibly on earth. The Millennium is for both Old Testament and New Testament believers. The curse is removed from the earth.	Jesus reigns now in the hearts of believers and through the church. There is no future literal Millennium on earth. This age ends with the Second Coming.	Jesus is leading the church in this present age to preach the Good News throughout the world. This preaching of the Good News will establish the Millennium on earth.
New Heaven and New Earth	The new heaven and new earth unites the two peoples of God, the Jews in their earthly millennium and Christians in their heavenly glory.	The new heaven and new earth introduce a new cosmos without the possibility of evil, where God is intimately present with his people.	The new heaven and new earth introduce a new cosmos without the possibility of evil, where God is intimately present with his people.	The new heaven and new earth introduce a new cosmos without the possibility of evil, where God is intimately present with his people.

DAY 8

Behold, the day of the LORD cometh,
and thy spoil shall be divided in the midst of thee.
For I will gather all nations against Jerusalem to battle;
and the city shall be taken, and the houses rifled,
and the women ravished; and half of the city shall go forth into captivity,
and the residue of the people shall not be cut off from the city.
Then shall the LORD go forth, and fight against those nations,
as when he fought in the day of battle. And his feet shall stand in that
day upon the mount of Olives, which is before Jerusalem on the east,
and the mount of Olives shall cleave in the midst thereof toward the east
and toward the west, and there shall be a very great valley; and half of
the mountain shall remove toward the north, and half of it toward the
south. And ye shall flee to the valley of the mountains; for the valley of
the mountains shall reach unto Azal: yea, ye shall flee, like as ye fled
from before the earthquake in the days of Uzziah king of Judah:
and the LORD my God shall come, and all the saints with thee.
ZECHARIAH 14:1–5

And when they shall have finished their testimony, the beast that ascend-
eth out of the bottomless pit shall make war against them, and shall
overcome them, and kill them. And their dead bodies shall lie in the
street of the great city, which spiritually is called Sodom and Egypt,
where also our Lord was crucified.
REVELATION 11:7–8

And he gathered them together into a place
called in the Hebrew tongue Armageddon.
REVELATION 16:16

DISPENSATIONAL PREMILLENNIAL VIEW

"And I heard the number of them which were sealed: and there were sealed an hundred and forty and four thousand of all the tribes of the children of Israel" (Revelation 7:4). The book of Revelation assigns the nation of Israel a central role in the events of the end times. In addition to describing the sealing of 144,000 Israelites, the Bible places several end-times events in the land of Israel: the two faithful witnesses will die in Jerusalem (Revelation 11:3–8), the armies of the world will gather near Israel in the last days (Zechariah 14:1–5; Revelation 16:16), and Jesus will return to the Mount of Olives (Zechariah 14:4).

Dispensational premillennialists take special note of Israel and its role in those final days. If Israelites are described as God's chosen people, why shouldn't the nation of Israel play a major role in end-time events? Dispensationalists believe the return of the Jews to Palestine, the reestablishment of the state of Israel in 1948, and its continuing prosperity in the face of on-going persecution can only be explained as miraculous. They're signs that the end is near.

Need to Know
- A *dispensation* is a period of time. When we use the word to describe a perspective on end times—dispensationalism—we are talking (at the most basic level) about an understanding of God dealing with man differently, progressively through different periods of time. An example would be the period of the Law of Moses, which was both affirmed and superceded by the grace that was revealed through Jesus Christ.
- A *premillennial* view is a belief that Christ will return to earth to gather believers *before* he reigns on the earth for one thousand years.

Think About It
- Do you see a distinct role between the nation of Israel and the church, or do you see Israel's role absorbed into the Christian church?
- What do you think the role of the church is in preparing for the end of the world as we know it?

Day 9

Seventy weeks are determined upon thy people and upon thy holy city,
to finish the transgression, and to make an end of sins,
and to make reconciliation for iniquity, and to bring in everlasting
righteousness, and to seal up the vision and prophecy,
and to anoint the most Holy. Know therefore and understand,
that from the going forth of the commandment to restore and to build
Jerusalem unto the Messiah the Prince shall be seven weeks,
and threescore and two weeks: the street shall be built again,
and the wall, even in troublous times. And after threescore and two
weeks shall Messiah be cut off, but not for himself: and the people
of the prince that shall come shall destroy the city and the sanctuary;
and the end thereof shall be with a flood, and unto the end of the war
desolations are determined. And he shall confirm the covenant with
many for one week: and in the midst of the week he shall
cause the sacrifice and the oblation to cease, and for the overspreading
of abominations he shall make it desolate, even until the consummation,
and that determined shall be poured upon the desolate.
DANIEL 9:24–27

Let us be glad and rejoice, and give honour to him:
for the marriage of the Lamb is come,
and his wife hath made herself ready.
And to her was granted that she should be arrayed
in fine linen, clean and white:
for the fine linen is the righteousness of saints.
And he saith unto me, Write,
Blessed are they which are called
unto the marriage supper of the Lamb.
And he saith unto me,
These are the true sayings of God.
REVELATION 19:7–9

Israel and the Church

Dispensational premillennialists divide God's plan for humanity into several eras or "dispensations." God has separate plans for Israel and the church. Dispensationalists point to God's promises to Abraham, David, and others that Israel would be physically and spiritually restored in Canaan under the Messiah's rule. These promises to Israel must never be confused with God's promises to the church. In contrast to Israel's promised earthly future, the church anticipates a heavenly existence as Christ's bride (Revelation 19:7–9). Israel and the church will experience separate second comings, resurrections, judgments, and future blessings.

Dispensationalists believe that Daniel's vision in Daniel 7 describes a seven-year period of tribulation designed to bring the Jews back to God. In Daniel's vision, the antichrist first befriends the Jews. Then after what dispensationalists interpret as three and a half years (Daniel 7:25), the antichrist begins persecuting the Jews (Daniel 7:8, 20–27; 9:24–27; see Matthew 24:15–22). As a result of this persecution, Jews will begin to return to God.

Need to Know
- Throughout the New Testament God describes his people as both the *body of Christ* and the *bride of Christ*. The church is Christ's body in that the church is the physical representation of Christ in the world. The church is Christ's bride in that she will be joined with him in a great wedding feast in eternity.
- While we all understand the terms *trials* and *tribulations,* what we usually call the *Great Tribulation* is a period of trouble and persecution that will be a specific part of the end-times scenario.

Think About It
- How do you feel you are prepared for a time of tribulation and persecution for those of the Christian faith?
- How do you function as a part of the body of Christ?

Day 10

*For other foundation can no man lay than that is laid,
which is Jesus Christ. Now if any man build upon this
foundation gold, silver, precious stones, wood, hay, stubble;
Every man's work shall be made manifest: for the day shall declare it,
because it shall be revealed by fire; and the fire shall try every man's work
of what sort it is. If any man's work abide which he hath built
thereupon, he shall receive a reward. If any man's work shall be burned,
he shall suffer loss: but he himself shall be saved; yet so as by fire.*

1 Corinthians 3:11–15

*For our conversation is in heaven; from whence also we look for
the Saviour, the Lord Jesus Christ: Who shall change our vile body,
that it may be fashioned like unto his glorious body, according to the
working whereby he is able even to subdue all things unto himself.*

Philippians 3:20–21

*Praise our God, all ye his servants, and ye that fear him,
both small and great. And I heard as it were the voice of a great
multitude, and as the voice of many waters, and as the voice of mighty
thunderings, saying, Alleluia: for the Lord God omnipotent reigneth.
Let us be glad and rejoice, and give honour to him: for the marriage of
the Lamb is come, and his wife hath made herself ready. And to her was
granted that she should be arrayed in fine linen, clean and white: for the
fine linen is the righteousness of saints. And he saith unto me, Write,
Blessed are they which are called unto the marriage supper of the Lamb.
And he saith unto me, These are the true sayings of God.*

Revelation 19:5–9

The Rapture

Dispensationalists point out that Scripture urges the church to watch only for Christ's return—not some other event, like the Tribulation (1 Corinthians 1:7; Philippians 3:20–21). As Paul writes, Christians await Jesus who "delivered us from the wrath to come" (1 Thessalonians 1:10; see also Revelation 6:16–17; 11:18). Simply put, dispensationalists believe that Jesus' return is imminent. He can come at anytime, and the church won't experience the Tribulation.

In the Rapture, all believers—both living and dead—will meet the Lord in midair and ascend to heaven. Transformed in their new bodies, believers will appear before the judgment seat of Christ for their rewards (1 Corinthians 3:11–15). Then the church as Christ's bride will enjoy the marriage supper of the Lamb (Revelation 19:1–9).

Need to Know
- The bride of Christ, the church, will be dressed in *white*. The Levites, worship leaders of the temple, also wore white linen. It was a symbol of holiness.
- The word *rapture* comes from a Greek word that means "to be caught up."

Think About It
- When you think of Christ's return, what are you most eager for or threatened by?
- When you think of appearing before the judgment seat of Christ, what thoughts come to mind?

Day 11

And he shall judge among the nations, and shall rebuke many people:
and they shall beat their swords into plowshares,
and their spears into pruninghooks: nation shall not lift up
sword against nation, neither shall they learn war any more.
ISAIAH 2:4

For unto us a child is born, unto us a son is given:
and the government shall be upon his shoulder:
and his name shall be called Wonderful, Counsellor,
The mighty God, The everlasting Father, The Prince of Peace.
Of the increase of his government and peace there shall be no end,
upon the throne of David, and upon his kingdom, to order it,
and to establish it with judgment and with justice from henceforth
even for ever. The zeal of the LORD of hosts will perform this.
ISAIAH 9:6–7

The wolf also shall dwell with the lamb,
and the leopard shall lie down with the kid;
and the calf and the young lion and the fatling together;
and a little child shall lead them. And the cow and the bear shall feed;
their young ones shall lie down together: and the lion shall eat straw
like the ox. And the sucking child shall play on the hole of the asp,
and the weaned child shall put his hand on the cockatrice's den.
They shall not hurt nor destroy in all my holy mountain: for the earth
shall be full of the knowledge of the LORD, as the waters cover the sea.
ISAIAH 11:6–9

CHRIST'S SECOND COMING AND MILLENNIAL REIGN

At the end of the Tribulation, Jesus will return to defeat his enemies at Armageddon, bind Satan, and establish himself as king over Israel (Revelation 19:19–20:6). The Old Testament believers and the martyrs of the Tribulation will be brought back to life. Jews and non-Jews, both living and dead, will be judged to ensure that only believers enter the millennial kingdom (Ezekiel 20:34–38; Daniel 12:2–3; Matthew 25:31–46; Revelation 20:4–6).

During the thousand-year reign of Christ, the Old Testament promises for Israel will be fulfilled. Christ will reign from Jerusalem on David's throne, establishing justice and peace over all nations (Isaiah 2:4; 9:6–7; 42:1). No longer cursed, the world will be free from sickness and disease (Isaiah 35:5–6). Even the hostility among animals will cease (Isaiah 11:6–9).

Need to Know
- The Hebrew word *Armageddon* actually means "Mount Megiddo." Megiddo is a town in northern Palestine. Because of its location, it has been the scene of many historical battles.
- The kingdom of Christ—a literal, physical, military kingdom—is what the Jews have looked forward to since the days described in the Old Testament. It is the basis of their misunderstanding of Christ's mission, which was first to establish a heavenly kingdom based on his sacrifice.

Think About It
- What are any fears you have, or you think others might have, about the return of Christ?
- What is most inviting to you about the millennial reign of Christ as described above?

Day 12

Be ye also patient; stablish your hearts:
for the coming of the Lord draweth nigh.
Grudge not one against another, brethren, lest ye be condemned:
behold, the judge standeth before the door.
JAMES 5:8–9

And the devil that deceived them was cast into the lake of fire
and brimstone, where the beast and the false prophet are,
and shall be tormented day and night for ever and ever.
REVELATION 20:10

And I saw a new heaven and a new earth: for the first heaven
and the first earth were passed away; and there was no more sea.
And I John saw the holy city, new Jerusalem, coming down from
God out of heaven, prepared as a bride adorned for her husband.
And I heard a great voice out of heaven saying, Behold, the tabernacle
of God is with men, and he will dwell with them, and they shall be
his people, and God himself shall be with them, and be their God.
And God shall wipe away all tears from their eyes;
and there shall be no more death, neither sorrow, nor crying, neither
shall there be any more pain: for the former things are passed away.
REVELATION 21:1–4

The New Heaven and New Earth

Dispensationalists believe the Millennium will end with Satan leading a brief rebellion against Christ. After he is defeated, Satan will be thrown into the lake of fire (Revelation 20:10). The remaining unsaved dead will be raised. Unlike believers, they will face judgment alone—without Christ. They will be judged solely on what they did while on earth.

God will then recreate the heavens and earth, eliminating any possibility of evil. Finally, he will bring together the believers in the heavenly church and the earthly Israel. The book of Revelation pictures the heavenly New Jerusalem descending to earth (Revelation 21:1–4). There, Jewish and non-Jewish believers will live with God.

Dispensational premillennialists repeatedly warn that Jesus could return at any moment. "The coming of the Lord draweth nigh. . .the judge standeth before the door" (James 5:8–9). Be ready for Jesus!

Need to Know
- The *lake of fire* is mentioned only in Revelation. It is the final resting place of Satan and those associated with him. It's probably the same place that Jesus referred to as Gehenna.
- *Gehenna* actually refers to a low valley bordering the tribal territories of Benjamin and Judah in ancient Israel. Infant sacrifices were carried out there, so it was considered a place of great evil.

Think About It
- What does it mean to you to be ready for Jesus' coming?
- What specifically do you need to accomplish in order to be prepared for Christ's return?

Day 13

I pray not that thou shouldest take them out of the world,
but that thou shouldest keep them from the evil.
JOHN 17:15

And if children, then heirs; heirs of God,
and joint-heirs with Christ; if so be that we suffer with him,
that we may be also glorified together.
ROMANS 8:17

And to wait for his Son from heaven,
whom he raised from the dead, even Jesus,
which delivered us from the wrath to come.
1 THESSALONIANS 1:10

Be patient therefore, brethren, unto the coming of the Lord.
Behold, the husbandman waiteth for the precious fruit of the earth,
and hath long patience for it, until he receive the early and latter rain.
Be ye also patient; stablish your hearts:
for the coming of the Lord draweth nigh.
JAMES 5:7–8

And I saw an angel standing in the sun;
and he cried with a loud voice, saying to all the fowls
that fly in the midst of heaven, Come and gather yourselves together
unto the supper of the great God; That ye may eat the flesh of kings,
and the flesh of captains, and the flesh of mighty men,
and the flesh of horses, and of them that sit on them,
and the flesh of all men, both free and bond, both small and great.
And I saw the beast, and the kings of the earth,
and their armies, gathered together to make war against him
that sat on the horse, and against his army.
And the beast was taken, and with him the false prophet
that wrought miracles before him, with which he deceived
them that had received the mark of the beast,
and them that worshipped his image.
These both were cast alive into a lake of fire burning with brimstone.
And the remnant were slain with the sword of him that
sat upon the horse, which sword proceeded out of his mouth:
and all the fowls were filled with their flesh.
REVELATION 19:17–21

Jesus' Second Coming

Jesus prophesied a future of persecution and catastrophe. This period of unprecedented evil will climax with the antichrist proclaiming himself to be deity, leading a worldwide rebellion against God, and ushering in a time of tremendous suffering and tribulation (Matthew 24:15–22; 2 Thessalonians 2:3–12). Historic premillennialists contend that Scripture doesn't promise an escape from the Tribulation, but instead calls Christians to be watchful, guarding themselves against spiritual compromise (James 5:7–8). Although Christians will experience the same type of suffering Christ experienced, God promises to spare them from his wrath (John 15:18; 17:15; Romans 8:17; 1 Thessalonians 1:10).

For historic premillennialists, the Second Coming is a supernatural event that will occur only after the Tribulation. They see two purposes for Christ's return: He will come to rescue believers and usher them into his millennial kingdom, and he will come to judge his enemies. Christ will defeat the opposing forces at Armageddon, condemning the antichrist to the lake of fire (Revelation 19:11–21). This will complete the first stage in Christ's conquest of his enemies. Jesus also will raise dead and living believers. These believers will have new bodies and meet Christ in the air to accompany him as he establishes his millennial kingdom on earth.

Need to Know
- First century Christians thought it an honor to suffer as Christ had. Paul referred to the "fellowship of his sufferings" (Philippians 3:10).
- *Persecution* is suffering specifically imposed because of a person's faith. Persecution of the righteous can be found throughout the Bible.

Think About It
- What thoughts do you have about the fact that God does not promise an escape from suffering for those who follow him?
- When you think of being judged by God, what areas most concern you?

Day 14

God is gone up with a shout, the Lord with the sound of a trumpet.
Sing praises to God, sing praises: sing praises unto our King, sing praises.
For God is the King of all the earth: sing ye praises with understanding.
God reigneth over the heathen: God sitteth upon the throne of his
holiness. The princes of the people are gathered together,
even the people of the God of Abraham:
for the shields of the earth belong unto God:
he is greatly exalted.
PSALM 47:5–9

And I saw an angel come down from heaven,
having the key of the bottomless pit and a great chain in his hand.
And he laid hold on the dragon, that old serpent,
which is the Devil, and Satan, and bound him a thousand years,
And cast him into the bottomless pit, and shut him up,
and set a seal upon him, that he should deceive the nations no more,
till the thousand years should be fulfilled:
and after that he must be loosed a little season.
REVELATION 20:1–3

JESUS' MILLENNIAL REIGN

Jesus will demonstrate his earthly rule by chaining Satan in the bottomless pit for a thousand years, preventing him from deceiving the nations anymore (Revelation 20:1–3). Premillennialists believe that the establishment of Christ's millennial reign on earth will spur the nation of Israel to turn to Jesus. Moreover, this millennial period will fulfill Old Testament prophecies of peace, righteousness, and extraordinary harmony between both people and nature—"The wolf shall also dwell with the lamb, and the leopard shall lie down with the kid; . . .and a little child shall lead them" (Isaiah 11:6–8; 35:1–10; see also Psalms 47 and 72).

Historic premillennialists assert that only believers will be raised from the dead to reign with Christ in the Millennium—the thousand years of peace and harmony. The remaining unbelieving dead will be raised to life when the Millennium ends (Revelation 20:4–5). At that time, Christ will sit on his great white throne to judge these unbelievers.

The Millennium will end with a daring rebellion against God himself. Satan will be released from the bottomless pit for a short time. He will deceive people and gather them from the ends of the world to fight against God (Revelation 20:8). But God will destroy these forces and condemn Satan to the lake of fire for all eternity.

Need to Know
- The Hebrew word translated as *bottomless pit,* actually means "the deep." Some translations use "the abyss."
- The book of Job gives insight into God's dealings with Satan. It portrays almost a courtroom-like setting in which Satan contests God and his followers (Job 1:6–12).

Think About It
- What works of Satan have you witnessed?
- What fears do you have regarding wickedness in this world? What comfort do you find in God?

Day 15

Then cometh the end, when he shall have delivered
up the kingdom to God, even the Father;
when he shall have put down all rule
and all authority and power.
For he must reign, till he hath put all enemies under his feet.
The last enemy that shall be destroyed is death.
1 Corinthians 15:24–26

That at the name of Jesus every knee should bow,
of things in heaven, and things in earth,
and things under the earth;
And that every tongue should confess
that Jesus Christ is Lord,
to the glory of God the Father.
Philippians 2:10–11

JESUS' SPIRITUAL REIGN

Historic premillennialists believe that Jesus currently rules as Lord in a spiritual way in the lives of believers and in the church. But Jesus' goal is to destroy "all rule and all authority and power" so that everything is under his control (1 Corinthians 15:24–25). Christ will conquer the antichrist, Satan, and then death itself. All creation will eventually acknowledge Jesus as Lord (Philippians 2:10–11).

Historic premillennialists believe that when the Millennium ends, the dead will be raised and every person will stand before the large, white throne of the Lord. This final judgment will determine everyone's eternal destiny, whether it be everlasting life or condemnation. Finally, God condemns death itself to the lake of fire. Then Christ reigns over all his enemies. At that point, God will bring into existence the new heaven and new earth. Creation once again will become whole. Evil will never resurface again.

Need to Know
- The first Old Testament evidence of the resurrection of the dead was in the book of Daniel, one of the later books written. Before that, death was referred to merely as the end of life without much comment on what happened beyond.
- Christ's resurrection gave obvious power to the understanding that our souls are eternal and live on beyond our bodies. This legacy beyond this life, beyond Satan's power and beyond our control, is the legacy of Christ.

Think About It
- What methods of operation in the modern world do you most look forward to replacing with the reign of Christ?
- What will life be like when justice is complete and death is no more?

Table: What Will Be Missing in Heaven?

What's Missing?	Why?	How Do We Know?
Death	God will destroy death.	Isaiah 25:8; 1 Corinthians 15:26; Revelation 21:4
Limits of time, space, and gravity	Jesus' resurrected body is a prototype of our resurrected body. His body didn't have the same limitations our bodies currently have.	Luke 24:31; John 20:19, 26
Judgment of sin	The curse of consequences for sin will be gone.	Revelation 22:3
Sun and moon	The glory of God will provide light all of the time.	Revelation 21:23
Night	God's glory will always illuminate heaven. The gates of New Jerusalem will never close because there will never be night.	Revelation 21:25; 22:5
Pain	God will make these "former things" disappear.	Revelation 21:4

What's Missing?	Why?	How Do We Know?
Seas	No reason given.	Revelation 21:1
Sickness	The tree of life will provide healing.	Revelation 22:2
Sin	Only those whose names are in the book of life will be there.	Revelation 21:27
Tears	God will wipe away every tear.	Revelation 7:17; 21:4
Temple	The Lord God and the Lamb will be our temple.	Revelation 21:22
Thirst and hunger	The Shepherd will meet all our needs.	Revelation 7:16–17

Day 16

Another parable put he forth unto them, saying,
The kingdom of heaven is like to a grain of mustard seed,
which a man took, and sowed in his field:
Which indeed is the least of all seeds: but when it is grown,
it is the greatest among herbs, and becometh a tree,
so that the birds of the air come and lodge in the branches thereof.
Another parable spake he unto them;
The kingdom of heaven is like unto leaven,
which a woman took, and hid in three measures of meal,
till the whole was leavened.
MATTHEW 13:31–33

And Jesus came and spake unto them, saying,
All power is given unto me in heaven and in earth.
Go ye therefore, and teach all nations, baptizing them
in the name of the Father, and of the Son, and of the Holy Ghost:
Teaching them to observe all things whatsoever I have commanded you:
and, lo, I am with you alway, even unto the end of the world. Amen.
MATTHEW 28:18–20

Which he wrought in Christ, when he raised him from the dead,
and set him at his own right hand in the heavenly places,
Far above all principality, and power, and might, and dominion,
and every name that is named, not only in this world,
but also in that which is to come: And hath put all things under his feet,
and gave him to be the head over all things to the church.
EPHESIANS 1:20–22

POSTMILLENNIALISTS

Christians who ascribe to postmillennialism believe that Jesus will return to just such a world—one that has been "Christianized," thoroughly changed by the work of the church. In summary, they believe the Millennium will be established by the efforts of Christians, and Christ will only return to the earth after the Millennium.

Postmillennialists believe that although Jesus is in heaven, he at the present time reigns as Lord over all creation (Acts 2:32–36; Ephesians 1:20–22). Since all power and authority has been given to Jesus, and since Jesus promised that he will be with his followers "unto the end of the world" (Matthew 28:18–20), postmillennialists contend that nothing can stop Christ's followers from carrying out their mission to evangelize the entire world.

The church is now gradually transforming society in the same way that yeast gradually permeates a loaf of bread (Matthew 13:33). Of course, the church's progress faces obstacles. Postmillennialists believe that John's vision of the Tribulation symbolizes the constant conflict between good and evil that has existed throughout history (Revelation 7:14; 13:1–18).

Need to Know
• The book of Acts is the story of the early church organizing itself to accomplish Jesus' commission to evangelize the world.
• The first-century Christians believed they were living in the end times just as many Christians do today. The fervency with which they worked is the same fervency with which modern Christians work, observing our culture and anticipating the redemption of the world.

Think About It
• How would you describe your hope that the modern church will "Christianize" the world?
• What do you feel is your call in the task of the church?

Day 17

And he shall judge among the nations,
and shall rebuke many people:
and they shall beat their swords into plowshares,
and their spears into pruninghooks:
nation shall not lift up sword against nation,
neither shall they learn war any more.

ISAIAH 2:4

And I saw thrones, and they sat upon them,
and judgment was given unto them: and I saw the souls
of them that were beheaded for the witness of Jesus,
and for the word of God, and which had not worshipped the beast,
neither his image, neither had received his mark
upon their foreheads, or in their hands;
and they lived and reigned with Christ a thousand years.
But the rest of the dead lived not again
until the thousand years were finished.
This is the first resurrection.
Blessed and holy is he that hath part in the first resurrection:
on such the second death hath no power,
but they shall be priests of God and of Christ,
and shall reign with him a thousand years.

REVELATION 20:4–6

THE POSTMILLENNIUM

Postmillennialists believe that the Millennium will occur within human history. The psalmist's vision that one day all nations will sing God's praise, that righteousness will flourish, and that true justice will reign will be fulfilled in our present age (Psalm 47; 72). The Good News of Christ has the power not only to bring about personal change, but social and cultural transformation as well. Swords will be hammered into plowshares (Isaiah 2:4), the desert will spring to life (Isaiah 35:1, 7), and Satan will be bound (Revelation 20:1–3).

Postmillennialists believe that this golden age of righteousness and prosperity will result not from Christ's visible earthly reign but from his invisible spiritual reign from heaven through his word (Revelation 19:11–21; 20:4–6). The Millennium will result from historical forces that are present now—not from cataclysmic or miraculous events. Similarly, postmillennialists interpret the "first resurrection" not as a promise that martyrs will receive new bodies, but that their cause in spreading the Good News will triumph (Revelation 20:4–6). They insist that the thousand years in Revelation 20:2 are symbolic of a perfect time—one that may last more than a thousand years.

Need to Know

- Numbers are often used symbolically in Scripture because that is how they were used in the ancient world. When Jesus told Peter to forgive someone seventy times seven times, he wasn't limiting forgiveness to 490 encounters. He was saying, "keep on forgiving indefinitely."
- In the late 1800s the Social Gospel movement combined social justice with the spread of the gospel. Current thinking often has us choose between the two rather than seeing Christ's holistic redemption.

Think About It

- How is your faith making the world around you a better place?
- What does it mean to you to see yourself as a part of God's redemptive work in the world?

TABLE: NUMBERS IN SCRIPTURE

Number	Symbolic Meaning	Sample Reference	Specific Significance
two	Related to witness or mutual support	Revelation 11:3	John depicts two powerful witnesses who will speak the Good News of Christ boldly to the world.
three	Related to unity or divinity	Revelation 4:8	Note the three-part praise for God: "Holy, holy, holy."
four	Related to earth	Revelation 6	There are four horsemen of the apocalypse.
six	Revelation 13:18	Revelation 6	The number of the antichrist is 666.
seven	Related to divine perfection	Revelation 1:12, 16; 5:1, 6; 8:2	Jesus wrote to seven churches. Seven golden candlesticks represented the churches. Christ holds seven stars in his hand. The book of judgment has seven seals. Seven angels declare judgments in sets of seven.
ten	Related to human government	Revelation 13:1; 17:12	Ten nations rise up in the final battle of Armageddon.
twelve	Related to divine rule or government	Revelation 7:4–8; 21:12–21	There are twelve tribes of Israel, and 144,000 are sealed by God's angel (12 times 12,000). There are also twelve foundations, layers, and gates for the New Jerusalem.

Day 18

And when the thousand years are expired,
Satan shall be loosed out of his prison,
And shall go out to deceive the nations
which are in the four quarters of the earth,
Gog and Magog, to gather them together to battle:
the number of whom is as the sand of the sea.
And they went up on the breadth of the earth,
and compassed the camp of the saints about, and the beloved city:
and fire came down from God out of heaven, and devoured them.
And the devil that deceived them was cast into the lake of fire
and brimstone, where the beast and the false prophet are,
and shall be tormented day and night for ever and ever.
REVELATION 20:7–10

And I saw a new heaven and a new earth:
for the first heaven and the first earth were passed away;
and there was no more sea. And I John saw the holy city, new Jerusalem,
coming down from God out of heaven, prepared as a bride adorned
for her husband. And I heard a great voice out of heaven saying,
Behold, the tabernacle of God is with men, and he will dwell with them,
and they shall be his people, and God himself shall be with them,
and be their God. And God shall wipe away all tears from their eyes;
and there shall be no more death, neither sorrow, nor crying, neither
shall there be any more pain: for the former things are passed away.
REVELATION 21:1–4

Jesus' Second Coming

Postmillennialists believe that the Millennium will end when Satan is released from the bottomless pit to launch a brief offensive (Revelation 20:7–10), then Christ will return to judge all people. Upon his return, the dead will be raised to face judgment (John 5:28–29). Christ will establish a new heaven and new earth, where evil will no longer exist (Revelation 21:1–22:5).

Postmillennialists are optimistic about the future of humanity only because Jesus Christ has changed the destiny of history. They believe the church bears the awesome responsibility of spreading the Good News to all the world. And it's the church's commitment to tell others about Jesus that will bring about that idyllic period of peace and prosperity—the Millennium.

Need to Know
- As early as the writings of the Old Testament prophet Isaiah, we can find the concept of the new heavens and new earth (Isaiah 65:17; 66:22). God promised redemption and restoration not just for his people, but for the world.
- In Jesus' closing remarks before his ascension, he gave the directive for his followers to spread the news of the gospel throughout the earth (Acts 1:8).

Think About It
- How does your optimism about the future of humanity compare to that of the postmillennialist?
- What problems, if any, do you have with this view of Christ's reign?

Day 19

And I appoint unto you a kingdom,
as my Father hath appointed unto me.
LUKE 22:29

Jesus answered, My kingdom is not of this world:
if my kingdom were of this world,
then would my servants fight,
that I should not be delivered to the Jews:
but now is my kingdom not from hence.
JOHN 18:36

Repent ye therefore, and be converted,
that your sins may be blotted out,
when the times of refreshing shall come from
the presence of the Lord;
And he shall send Jesus Christ,
which before was preached unto you:
Whom the heaven must receive until
the times of restitution of all things,
which God hath spoken by the mouth of
all his holy prophets since the world began.
ACTS 3:19–21

Who gave himself for our sins,
that he might deliver us from this present evil world,
according to the will of God and our Father.

Which he wrought in Christ,
when he raised him from the dead,
and set him at his own right hand in the heavenly places,
Far above all principality, and power, and might,
and dominion, and every name that is named,
not only in this world, but also in that which is to come:
And hath put all things under his feet,
and gave him to be the head over all things to the church,
Which is his body, the fulness of him that filleth all in all.

EPHESIANS 1:20–23

AMILLENNIALISTS AND THE KINGDOM OF GOD

Amillennialists see the Millennium as Christ's current reign over his church. They point out that the New Testament speaks of only two different ages—this present world and the world to come (Matthew 12:32; Mark 10:30; Luke 18:30; 20:34, John 16:11; Acts 3:19–21; 2 Corinthians 4:4; Hebrews 6:5). Because Satan is the "prince of this world" (John 16:11), the people of this age follow their worldly desires (Ephesians 2:2). In the world to come sinners will be punished for their evil, and the righteous will live forever (Matthew 12:36; 25:31–46). The event that divides these two ages is Christ's second coming.

Amillennialists believe that Jesus' work on the cross two thousand years ago established the kingdom of God. As a result, this "present evil world" (Galatians 1:4) is now passing away (1 Corinthians 7:31). Jesus bound Satan (Matthew 12:29), curtailing his power (Luke 10:17–19). Therefore, the "prince of this world" cannot prevent the spread of the Good News of Christ (Matthew 16:18). Jesus is now Lord, reigning as king in the hearts of believers (Luke 22:29; John 18:36; Ephesians 1:20–23). That's how Christ rules today. His kingdom is spiritual; it is the church.

Need to Know
- Jesus compared the kingdom of God to many things such as leaven, a grain of mustard seed, a treasure, a net, a marriage, and maidens waiting for the bridegroom (Matthew 13; Luke 13).
- Jesus' work on the cross was the redemption of humanity. Through his death, he paid for sin in the lives of people and provided a connection between God and humanity.

Think About It
- How would you define the kingdom of God?
- Do you believe you are already in that kingdom, or that you are waiting to be a part of it in eternity?

Timeline for the

 Jesus is now Lord

Jesus' Resurrection

Church Age

Church Age

- Jesus reigns in heaven, in the church, and in the hearts of believers.

- The millennium is now.

- Satan cannot stop the spread of the Good News.

- Hostility to Christians will gradually increase during the Church Age.

Amillennial View

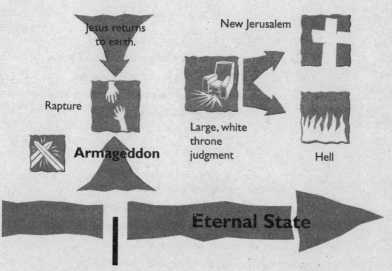

Jesus returns to earth.

New Jerusalem

Rapture

Armageddon

Large, white throne judgment

Hell

Eternal State

Christ's Second Coming

- Believers meet Jesus in midair.
- Believers descend with Christ to earth.
- Jesus defeats the antichrist at Armageddon.
- Jesus holds everyone accountable at the large, white throne judgment.

Eternity

- Believers go to the New Jerusalem.
- Unbelievers go to hell.

Day 20

Marvel not at this: for the hour is coming,
in the which all that are in the graves shall hear his voice,
And shall come forth; they that have done good,
unto the resurrection of life; and they that have done evil,
unto the resurrection of damnation.
John 5:28–29

Now we beseech you, brethren,
by the coming of our Lord Jesus Christ,
and by our gathering together unto him,
That ye be not soon shaken in mind,
or be troubled, neither by spirit, nor by word,
nor by letter as from us, as that the day of Christ is at hand.
Let no man deceive you by any means: for that day shall not come,
except there come a falling away first,
and that man of sin be revealed, the son of perdition;
2 Thessalonians 2:1–3

And I saw thrones, and they sat upon them,
and judgment was given unto them:
and I saw the souls of them that were beheaded
for the witness of Jesus, and for the word of God,
and which had not worshipped the beast,
neither his image, neither had received his mark upon their foreheads,
or in their hands; and they lived and reigned
with Christ a thousand years.
But the rest of the dead lived not again until
the thousand years were finished. This is the first resurrection.
Blessed and holy is he that hath part in the first resurrection:
on such the second death hath no power,
but they shall be priests of God and of Christ,
and shall reign with him a thousand years.
REVELATION 20:4–6

A Future Millennium and the End of This Age

Amillennialists insist that the idea of a thousand-year "golden era" is incompatible with this evil world. They believe that the various visions in the book of Revelation run parallel with each other (Revelation 5–20). In other words, Revelation is not organized chronologically. Each vision portrays spiritual realities in the *entire* church age. The last section of the book, Revelation 21–22, describes the age to come. According to amillennialists, the first resurrection described in Revelation 20:4–6 refers to dead believers reigning with Christ in heaven. After all, John sees only souls, not resurrected bodies, in this text. So the events of the Millennium described in Revelation 20:1–6 are actually occurring now!

Amillennialists believe that as the last days approach, the forces of evil will climax with the antichrist and the tribulation he brings (2 Thessalonians 2:1–3). On the "day of the Lord," Christ will descend to earth, gather those who belong to him, and raise the dead. At this glorious return, everyone will appear before the judgment seat of Christ. The righteous will be raised to life, and the wicked to judgment (John 5:28–29). Those who belong to Christ will live with him in everlasting glory.

Need to Know
- The phrase the "day of the lord" is used throughout Scripture, as early as the eighth-century B.C. prophet, Amos. It points to *the* day, as well as any day, that the Lord intervenes in history. Most often that intervention has to do with judgment, an accounting.
- A judgment seat was literally the place where a judge sat. Pilate was sitting on his judgment seat when his wife warned him about Jesus (Matthew 27:19). The judgment seat of Christ represents not so

much a place, as the absolute accountability that Christians will have before God.

Think About It
- What do you see as your role today in the kingdom of God?
- What does the hope of Christ's return offer to your life right now?

Table: Being Prepared

In the absence of a specific timetable, how should we live in the face of Christ's imminent return? As you might expect, the Bible has plenty to say on the subject.

What Should We Do?	Reference
Communicate God's Word as if we're running out of time.	2 Timothy 4:1–2
Control the tendency to judge others by reflecting on the final judgment.	1 Corinthians 4:5
Develop patience as we eagerly await the Lord's return.	James 5:8
Gather faithfully and regularly with other believers.	Hebrews 10:25
Maintain a pure life.	1 John 3:2–3
Remember Jesus' death, resurrection, and return when we take communion.	1 Corinthians 11:26
Lead others to Christ's mercy.	Jude 1:21–23
Take and give comfort based on Christ's imminent return.	1 Thessalonians 4:16, 18
Think about heaven.	Colossians 3:1–4
Love others.	1 Thessalonians 3:12–13

Day 21

Therefore being by the right hand of God exalted,
and having received of the Father the promise of the Holy Ghost,
he hath shed forth this, which ye now see and hear.
For David is not ascended into the heavens: but he saith himself,
The Lord said unto my Lord, Sit thou on my right hand,
Until I make thy foes thy footstool.
Therefore let all the house of Israel know assuredly,
that God hath made that same Jesus,
whom ye have crucified, both Lord and Christ.
ACTS 2:33–36

For he is not a Jew, which is one outwardly;
neither is that circumcision, which is outward in the flesh:
But he is a Jew, which is one inwardly;
and circumcision is that of the heart,
in the spirit, and not in the letter;
whose praise is not of men, but of God.
ROMANS 2:28–29

And if ye be Christ's, then are ye Abraham's seed,
and heirs according to the promise.
GALATIANS 3:29

What About Israel?

What about God's covenant with Israel? Isn't God faithful to his promises to Israel—for instance, that David's throne would be established forever? Amillennialists believe that the church—the true Israel—will fulfill these promises. Paul and John state that believers in Christ are Abraham's seed—the true Jews—and therefore heirs of God's promises (Romans 2:28–29; Galatians 3:29; Revelation 2:9; 3:9). Peter claims that the resurrected and ascended Jesus is now enthroned, fulfilling God's promise to David (Acts 2:33–36).

Where is the church's promised Jerusalem? It is the New Jerusalem that descends from heaven in Revelation's grand vision of the new heaven and new earth (Revelation 21–22; see Galatians 4:25–26; Hebrews 12:22–23). Here evil can never exist. "Waters of life" flow from the Lamb's throne, symbolizing God's intimate presence with his people. So amillennialists insist the church has displaced Israel.

Amillennialism presents the most straightforward view of the end times. On this earth, the wicked will continue to gather strength, persecuting believers more and more. Only when Christ returns, will wickedness be stopped once and for all. After judging both the living and dead, Christ will establish his everlasting reign of peace.

Need to Know
- The Old Testament is the story of the nation of Israel. It is the backdrop of the New Testament in which Jesus' very existence was interpreted through God's promise to Israel of a Messiah.
- God made many promises about the restoration of Israel. That's why the fate of Israel matters in any view of the end times. How will God fulfill those promises that have been made since ancient history?

Think About It
- What is the task of the church today?
- What is the responsibility of the church, if any, toward the descendants of Abraham?

DAY 22

Seventy weeks are determined upon thy people and upon thy holy city,
to finish the transgression, and to make an end of sins, and to make
reconciliation for iniquity, and to bring in everlasting righteousness,
and to seal up the vision and prophecy, and to anoint the most Holy.
Know therefore and understand, that from the going forth
of the commandment to restore and to build Jerusalem unto the Messiah
the Prince shall be seven weeks, and threescore and two weeks:
the street shall be built again, and the wall, even in troublous times.
And after threescore and two weeks shall Messiah be cut off,
but not for himself: and the people of the prince that shall come
shall destroy the city and the sanctuary; and the end thereof shall be
with a flood, and unto the end of the war desolations are determined.
And he shall confirm the covenant with many for one week:
and in the midst of the week he shall cause the sacrifice
and the oblation to cease, and for the overspreading of abominations
he shall make it desolate, even until the consummation,
and that determined shall be poured upon the desolate.
DANIEL 9:24–27

For then shall be great tribulation,
such as was not since the beginning of the world to this time,
no, nor ever shall be.
And except those days should be shortened,
there should no flesh be saved:
but for the elect's sake those days shall be shortened.
MATTHEW 24:21–22

Daniel's Seventy Weeks

Jesus described to his disciples a period of terrible suffering that would precede his second coming (Matthew 24:21–22). The disciples knew about this period of intense suffering—the Tribulation. Although a host of experts have tried to map out what will occur in the Tribulation, we don't know much more about this time than Jesus' disciples did two thousand years ago. Each expert—whether dispensationalist, premillennialist, or amillennialist—has his or her own unique interpretation of the events.

A discussion of the Tribulation usually begins with Daniel's prophecies of the seventy time periods, or "seventy weeks" (Daniel 9:24–27). For dispensational premillennialists, the prophecy of the seventieth week sets the framework for the Tribulation. It's in that "week" that Daniel predicts the establishment of what one translation of the Bible calls the "disgusting things" and another calls the "abomination of desolation" (Daniel 9:27). Many dispensationalists believe the antichrist will set up disgusting sacrilegious things in the rebuilt temple in Jerusalem, and for this reason and others they understand Daniel's prophecy as predicting a seven-year period of tribulation.

Need to Know
- Most agree that the "abomination of desolation" will be an object set up for people to worship in place of God.
- While we think of a week as seven days, the "weeks" Daniel referred to could be years or sets of years.

Think About It
- How important does it seem to you to understand more about the possible anatomy of the Tribulation? Why?
- Why do you think, in God's scheme of things, the details can seem so unclear about all this?

TABLE: PERSPECTIVES ON DANIEL'S SEVENTY WEEKS

Theory	Starting Point	Key Events of the First Sixty-Nine Weeks	Key Events of the Seventieth Week
Traditional	Commands to restore and rebuild Jerusalem, issued by Cyrus and Artaxerxes (Ezra 1; 6–7; Nehemiah 2)	(1) Jerusalem is continually restored, even during "troublous times" (Daniel 9:25). (2) Messiah is on the scene at the close of the time period.	(1) The last week begins as Jesus begins his public ministry. (2) Jesus dies at the three-and-a-half year (day) mark, and then, three and a half years (days) later, with Paul's conversion, God includes the Gentiles in the plan of salvation.
Dispensational	Commands to restore and rebuild Jerusalem, issued by Cyrus and Artaxerxes (Ezra 1; 6–7; Nehemiah 2)	(1) Jerusalem is continually restored, even during the "troublous times" (Daniel 9:25). (2) Messiah enters Jerusalem triumphantly and then is killed to end the time period.	(1) The last week is "on hold," pending God's removal of all believers and the initiation of the closing days of the Tribulation in the world, a period of seven years of judgment. (2) The last week begins with the rise of the antichrist. (3) After three and a half years, the antichrist violates a treaty with Israel and sets into motion the events that close history.

Day 23

And the rest of the men which were not killed by these plagues
yet repented not of the works of their hands,
that they should not worship devils,
and idols of gold, and silver, and brass, and stone,
and of wood: which neither can see, nor hear, nor walk:
Neither repented they of their murders, nor of their sorceries,
nor of their fornication, nor of their thefts.
REVELATION 9:20–21

And the sixth angel poured out his vial upon the great river Euphrates;
and the water thereof was dried up,
that the way of the kings of the east might be prepared.
And I saw three unclean spirits like frogs come out of the mouth of the
dragon, and out of the mouth of the beast,
and out of the mouth of the false prophet.
For they are the spirits of devils, working miracles, which go forth
unto the kings of the earth and of the whole world,
to gather them to the battle of that great day of God Almighty.
Behold, I come as a thief.
Blessed is he that watcheth, and keepeth his garments,
lest he walk naked, and they see his shame.
And he gathered them together into a place called
in the Hebrew tongue Armageddon.
REVELATION 16:12–16

Rapture, Judgments, Armageddon

Depending on whether you are a pretribulationist, posttribulationist, or midtribulationist, the Rapture will occur either at the beginning, middle, or end of the Tribulation. It's within those seven awful years of tribulation that many dispensationalists place Revelation's seven seal, trumpet, and bowl judgments; everything from the sun turning dark to a plague of painful boils occurs during these dreadful seven years. But even though a third of the earth will be completely devastated in seven short years, people will still refuse to turn to God (Revelation 9:20–21). They will gather together at Armageddon to fight against the Almighty (Revelation 16:12–16). It's at that time that Christ will appear to defeat his enemies and to set the stage for his final judgment. The details of all these events—how they will be fulfilled and when—are still being debated. No one knows exactly what will happen. Scripture does make it clear that though we may experience troubles on this earth, Jesus will ultimately rescue his people from their persecutors (1 Thessalonians 1:10).

Need to Know
- The Tribulation is generally agreed to be seven years divided in half by significant events. The disagreement described above is at what point, in relation to the Tribulation, Jesus will "take up" the believers from the struggle.
- In John's vision judgments were poured out on the earth. First, seals were broken, some of which were followed by horses of symbolic colors. Other judgments were heralded by trumpets, then poured out from bowls or vials.

Think About It
- From what you've read and studied, are you a pre-, post-, or midtribulationist? Why?
- What have you faced or witnessed in your life that shows that people can experience events convincing them of God's presence, yet still turn against him?

Day 24

And at that time shall Michael stand up,
the great prince which standeth for the children of thy people:
and there shall be a time of trouble,
such as never was since there was a nation even to that same time:
and at that time thy people shall be delivered,
every one that shall be found written in the book.
Daniel 12:1

Seeing it is a righteous thing with God
to recompense tribulation to them that trouble you;
And to you who are troubled rest with us,
when the Lord Jesus shall be revealed from heaven
with his mighty angels,
In flaming fire taking vengeance on them
that know not God, and that obey
not the gospel of our Lord Jesus Christ:
Who shall be punished with everlasting destruction
from the presence of the Lord,
and from the glory of his power;
When he shall come to be glorified in his saints,
and to be admired in all them that believe
(because our testimony among you was believed) in that day.
2 Thessalonians 1:6–10

Because thou hast kept the word of my patience,
I also will keep thee from the hour of temptation,
which shall come upon all the world,
to try them that dwell upon the earth.

REVELATION 3:10

And I said unto him, Sir, thou knowest.
And he said to me,
These are they which came out of great tribulation,
and have washed their robes,
and made them white in the blood of the Lamb.

REVELATION 7:14

WHY WORRY ABOUT THE TRIBULATION?

How would you like to live in a world plagued by catastrophes? A great earthquake? Meteorites falling to the earth? Fiery hail? And on top of that, all kinds of violence—skirmishes, battles, and wars?

The Bible speaks of just that type of terrible suffering—a period of evil unequaled in all of history (Daniel 12:1; Matthew 24:16–22; 2 Thessalonians 2:3–12; Revelation 7:14). It's the time when God's wrath will be unleashed against his enemies (2 Thessalonians 1:6–10; Revelation 6:1–17). Revelation describes this period when God orders his bowls of wrath to be poured on the world as a time of testing (Revelation 3:10; 8:1–9:21; 16:1–21).

While most Christians acknowledge the reality of the Tribulation, there is still considerable debate concerning when it will occur and who will be affected by it.

Need to Know
- Throughout history, the Jews interpreted God's love for them, in part, by his vengeance on their enemies. John represents God as this kind of champion as well.
- Michael, an archangel that appeared to Daniel, is also mentioned in Jude 1:9 (as the archangel) and in Revelation 12:7 (as a warring angel).

Think About It
- How do you think your faith would hold up in a time of great testing?
- What kind of work does God do in your life when you face a horrible struggle?

Day 25

And he shall speak great words against the most High,
and shall wear out the saints of the most High,
and think to change times and laws: and they shall be given into
his hand until a time and times and the dividing of time.
But the judgment shall sit, and they shall take away his dominion,
to consume and to destroy it unto the end.
And the kingdom and dominion, and the greatness of the kingdom
under the whole heaven, shall be given to the people of the saints
of the most High, whose kingdom is an everlasting kingdom,
and all dominions shall serve and obey him.

DANIEL 7:25–27

Immediately after the tribulation of those days shall the sun be darkened,
and the moon shall not give her light, and the stars shall fall
from heaven, and the powers of the heavens shall be shaken:
And then shall appear the sign of the Son of man in heaven:
and then shall all the tribes of the earth mourn, and they shall
see the Son of man coming in the clouds of heaven
with power and great glory.
And he shall send his angels with a great sound of a trumpet,
and they shall gather together his elect from the four winds,
from one end of heaven to the other.

MATTHEW 24:29–31

And to wait for his Son from heaven, whom he raised from the dead,
even Jesus, which delivered us from the wrath to come.

1 THESSALONIANS 1:10

DISPENSATIONAL PREMILLENNIAL VIEW OF ISRAEL

Dispensational premillennialists believe that Jesus' prophecy of a future tribulation will affect Israel, not the church. They point out that the antichrist is an integral part of Daniel's prophecy concerning the seventieth week, and according to dispensationalists, this prophecy only deals with God's plans for Israel (Daniel 9:27; Matthew 24:15–22). So according to the dispensational view, believers won't have to go through the Tribulation. Jesus will rescue them "from God's coming anger" (1 Thessalonians 1:10). Prior to the Tribulation, the church will be raptured out of the world when Christ suddenly descends from the clouds.

The rise of the antichrist begins a seven-year period of tribulation designed to bring Israel back to God. In Daniel's seventieth week, the antichrist first befriends Israel. Then after three and a half years, the antichrist blasphemes the all-powerful God by placing a sacrilegious thing in the temple. Afterwards, he persecutes the Jews with vengeance (Daniel 7:8, 20–27; 9:24–27; Matthew 24:15–22). During this period of unspeakable suffering, many Jews recognize Christ as the Messiah and begin to turn back to God. After these seven years of horror, Christ returns to defeat his enemies at Armageddon and begin his thousand-year reign of peace (Matthew 24:29–31).

Need to Know
- The Jews of Jesus' day rejected him as Messiah for a variety of reasons, but perhaps most of all because he didn't bring the earthly kingdom they expected from the champion God had promised to send. Today, Jews who have come to believe in Jesus are often called *Messianic* Jews.
- After Pentecost, when Christianity was first growing as a movement, it was a Jewish movement. As the early leaders decided that a person didn't have to become a Jew to become a Christian, the two became more separate.

Think About It

- Do you believe that God still has a separate plan for the Jews (as presented in the Old Testament) or that the Christian church now represents "God's chosen people" the way the Jewish nation once did?
- What signs or events do you see around you now that could represent a coming period of tribulation or persecution?

Day 26

Let no man deceive you by any means: for that day shall not come, except there come a falling away first, and that man of sin be revealed, the son of perdition; Who opposeth and exalteth himself above all that is called God, or that is worshipped; so that he as God sitteth in the temple of God, shewing himself that he is God. Remember ye not, that, when I was yet with you, I told you these things? And now ye know what withholdeth that he might be revealed in his time. For the mystery of iniquity doth already work: only he who now letteth will let, until he be taken out of the way. And then shall that Wicked be revealed, whom the Lord shall consume with the spirit of his mouth, and shall destroy with the brightness of his coming: Even him, whose coming is after the working of Satan with all power and signs and lying wonders, And with all deceivableness of unrighteousness in them that perish; because they received not the love of the truth, that they might be saved. And for this cause God shall send them strong delusion, that they should believe a lie: That they all might be damned who believed not the truth, but had pleasure in unrighteousness.

2 Thessalonians 2:3–12

Historic Premillennial View

Historic premillennialists see the Tribulation as the climactic manifestation of evil at the end of history. During that time the antichrist will proclaim himself to be god and launch a worldwide campaign of persecution of Christians (Matthew 24:15–22; 2 Thessalonians 2:3–12). According to historic premillennialists, Christians will go through this tribulation and will suffer for the cause of Jesus, but Jesus will sustain his people and protect them from God's dreadful judgments on the antichrist and his followers. Then at the height of this period of persecution, Christ will return to defeat his enemies at Armageddon and establish his thousand-year reign.

Need to Know

- Persecution was a familiar concept to the early Christians. Jesus' followers had been persecuted from the beginning of the Christian movement. In fact, at times they were charged with and persecuted for atheism, because they failed to recognize *all* the gods of the day.
- Saul of Tarsus, who later became Paul the apostle, was one of the original first-century bounty hunters looking for and putting to death any rogue Christians out spreading the word. After his conversion, Paul became a martyr for the faith he once tried to obliterate.

Think About It

- What persecution have you experienced or witnessed?
- What type of persecution do you fear the most?

TIMELINE FOR THE

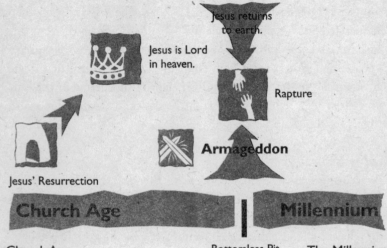

Jesus returns to earth.

Jesus is Lord in heaven.

Rapture

Armageddon

Jesus' Resurrection

Church Age | **Millennium**

Church Age

- Church spreads the Good News.
- There will be a period of tribulation towards the end of the church age.

Bottomless Pit

The Millennium

- Jesus physically rules on earth for 1,000 years.

Christ's Second Coming

- Christ defeats the antichrist at Armageddon.
- Believers meet Christ in midair.
- Believers descend to earth to reign with Jesus in the millennial kingdom.
- Satan is thrown in the bottomless pit.

Historic Premillennial View

Large, white
throne
judgment

New
Jerusalem

Hell

Great Rebellion

(1,000 Years) **Eternal State**

End of the Millennium

- At the end of the millennium, Satan is released.
- Jesus defeats the army Satan has gathered.
- All the dead are raised to face judgment.

Eternity

- Believers go to the New Jerusalem.
- Unbelievers go to hell.

Day 27

*And he shall send his angels with a great sound of a trumpet,
and they shall gather together his elect from the four winds,
from one end of heaven to the other.*
MATTHEW 24:31

*And one of the elders answered, saying unto me,
What are these which are arrayed in white robes?
and whence came they?
And I said unto him, Sir, thou knowest.
And he said to me,
These are they which came out of great tribulation,
and have washed their robes,
and made them white in the blood of the Lamb.*
REVELATION 7:13–14

Amillennial View

Amillennialists expect the battle between good and evil to climax in a period of intense persecution of Christians at the end of the age, just prior to Jesus' second coming. They believe the Tribulation isn't confined simply to the future, but is present in this age as well. The Tribulation occurs anywhere the Good News message is being opposed and Christians are being persecuted. Amillennialists point out that Scripture doesn't state that the Tribulation is confined to Israel (Revelation 7:13–14). They believe all of God's people will be persecuted. When Christ returns bringing judgment on evil, he will gather believers from every direction under the sky (Matthew 24:31).

Need to Know
- It is a powerful image. . .to wash robes in blood and see them turn white and clean. That is the picture of redemption and the purification of persecution described in Revelation 7. Jesus' blood cleanses our consciences (Hebrews 9:14) and gives us God's approval (Romans 3:21–22).
- John wrote Revelation toward the end of the first century. It was a time of growing unrest and tension between church and state. Rome's rule required worship of the emperor as well as allegiance. Refusal to offer up that worship was cause for intense persecution. John didn't have to look far to understand what tribulation was all about.

Think About It
- What contemporary persecution are you aware of around the world?
- Why do you think, in our modern age, people are still persecuted for the way they think and believe?

Day 28

If the world hate you, ye know that it hated me before it hated you.
JOHN 15:18

These things I have spoken unto you, that in me ye might have peace.
In the world ye shall have tribulation: but be of good cheer;
I have overcome the world.
JOHN 16:33

And not only so, but we glory in tribulations also:
knowing that tribulation worketh patience.
ROMANS 5:3

And if children, then heirs; heirs of God,
and joint-heirs with Christ;
if so be that we suffer with him,
that we may be also glorified together.
ROMANS 8:17

And to wait for his Son from heaven, whom he raised from the dead,
even Jesus, which delivered us from the wrath to come.
1 THESSALONIANS 1:10

POSTMILLENNIALISTS AND THE TRIBULATION

Postmillennialists believe the church itself will usher in the Millennium, and deny the idea of a future tribulation. They believe Jesus' prophecy of the sacrilege placed in the temple has already been fulfilled in Rome's destruction of Jerusalem and its temple in A.D. 70 (Matthew 24:15–22). They don't believe Jesus' prophecy speaks of a future antichrist.

Although people debate whether Christians will go through a time of terrible suffering, we must be ready to suffer for Jesus' sake. Jesus himself warned his disciples that they would experience all types of difficulties and hardships in this world (John 15:18–20; 16:33). As followers of Christ, we can expect trials and tribulations in our lives, but God promises that he won't desert us (John 15:18; 17:15; Romans 8:17; 1 Thessalonians 1:10). If our hope and trust is in Christ, we don't have to fear the future—no matter what it holds.

Need to Know
- Rome ruled Palestine from around A.D. 44 through A.D. 66. The Jews rebelled against Roman rule for four years until A.D. 70, when Jerusalem was attacked by the armies of Emperor Titus and her people butchered. The temple, just finally completed by Herod a few years earlier, was destroyed.
- The English word for "tribulation" comes from Latin word *tribulum,* "a threshing sledge," giving the idea of tightness, a pressing together. The majority of biblical references to tribulation are to the sufferings of God's people.

Think About It
- How would it change your view of the end times to believe that many of the events John described had already taken place in the first century?
- In what ways do you believe the Christians of your current culture are unprepared for suffering?

DAY 29

The LORD is slow to anger, and great in power,
and will not at all acquit the wicked:
the LORD hath his way in the whirlwind and in the storm,
and the clouds are the dust of his feet.

NAHUM 1:3

The Lord is not slack concerning his promise,
as some men count slackness; but is longsuffering to us-ward,
not willing that any should perish,
but that all should come to repentance.

2 PETER 3:9

THE JUDGMENT OF GOD

In his grace and goodness, God has been withholding his judgment for thousands of years. The apostle Peter describes it this way: "The Lord is not slack concerning his promise, as some men count slackness; but is longsuffering to us-ward, not willing that any should perish, but that all should come to repentance" (2 Peter 3:9). God has been more than fair with humankind.

When the time comes for God's holy judgment though, his punishment will be swift and complete. We need to look no further than the book of Revelation for evidence of that. Nahum, an Old Testament prophet, offers an apt description of God: "The LORD is slow to anger, and great in power, and will not at all acquit the wicked" (Nahum 1:3).

Need to Know
- Nahum was the prophet who predicted the downfall of Nineveh and the nation for which it was the capital, Assyria. This was the same Nineveh that Jonah had been called to preach to years before.
- God's judgment and humanity's accountability to him has been a part of the story since Adam and Eve disobeyed God in the Garden of Eden. Part of what makes the end-times judgment of God seem so much harsher is the finality of it. The same judgment of sin and death was introduced in Eden, but the actuality of that judgment will be bitter.

Think About It
- In what ways do you feel accountable to God on a daily basis?
- How does your hope in Christ affect how you think of God's final judgment?

Day 30

*Seventy weeks are determined upon thy people and upon thy holy city,
to finish the transgression, and to make an end of sins, and to make
reconciliation for iniquity, and to bring in everlasting righteousness,
and to seal up the vision and prophecy, and to anoint the most Holy.*

DANIEL 9:24

*And straightway coming up out of the water, he saw the heavens opened,
and the Spirit like a dove descending upon him:
And there came a voice from heaven, saying,
Thou art my beloved Son, in whom I am well pleased.*

MARK 1:10–11

*The Spirit of the Lord is upon me, because he hath anointed me to
preach the gospel to the poor; he hath sent me to heal the brokenhearted,
to preach deliverance to the captives, and recovering of sight to the blind,
to set at liberty them that are bruised.*

LUKE 4:18

*God, who at sundry times and in divers manners spake in time past
unto the fathers by the prophets, Hath in these last days spoken
unto us by his Son, whom he hath appointed heir of all things,
by whom also he made the worlds; Who being the brightness of his glory,
and the express image of his person, and upholding all things
by the word of his power, when he had by himself purged our sins,
sat down on the right hand of the Majesty on high.*

HEBREWS 1:1–3

THE TRADITIONAL VIEW

Many Christians believe that Daniel's seventy weeks were fulfilled in Jesus' first coming, and that there are no future events in Daniel 9. They believe Jesus fulfilled all six purposes of Daniel's seventy weeks (Daniel 9:24). They contend that Christ's death paid the penalty for our sin, bringing an "end of sin," rebellion, and guilt (Hebrews 9:26; 10:12–14). Moreover, Jesus established our "everlasting righteousness" by his death on the cross (Romans 3:21–22; 5:17–18). They suggest that "sealing the vision and prophecy" refers to the coming of Christ, the final Prophet (Acts 3:22; Hebrew 1:1–3). They interpret the sixth purpose, "anoint the Most Holy," as predicting the Holy Spirit's anointing of Jesus at his baptism (Mark 1:10–11; Luke 4:18).

Need to Know
- To review, in response to Daniel's prayer about Jerusalem, God sent the angel Gabriel, with a prophecy about seventy time periods, translated *weeks* by some. The interpretation of this prophecy has become a bedrock of end-times interpretations.
- Before Jesus came, there were prophets of God who spoke God's truth and foretold the future. Most of their prophecies looked forward to the Messiah, who would be sent from God to save his people. After Jesus' life, death, and resurrection, we look back to the story of Jesus to learn how to live. Jesus was the final prophet in that regard.

Think About It
- What would it mean for your view of the end times to believe that Daniel's prophecies were already accomplished in Christ?
- What did Christ's death accomplish in your life?

Day 31

*And after threescore and two weeks shall Messiah be cut off,
but not for himself: and the people of the prince
that shall come shall destroy the city and the sanctuary;
and the end thereof shall be with a flood,
and unto the end of the war desolations are determined.
And he shall confirm the covenant with many for one week:
and in the midst of the week he shall cause the sacrifice
and the oblation to cease, and for the overspreading of abominations
he shall make it desolate, even until the consummation,
and that determined shall be poured upon the desolate.*

DANIEL 9:26–27

FULFILLED IN CHRIST

Though it's unclear from the text whether Jerusalem's destruction and the defilement of the temple (Daniel 9:26–27) belong within Daniel's seventy weeks, the traditional view states that these two events were fulfilled when Titus destroyed the temple in A.D. 70. So according to the traditionalists, everything Daniel predicted in the seventieth week has already been fulfilled.

These two different ways of interpreting Daniel's seventy weeks (already fulfilled or yet to be fulfilled) are clearly at odds. But at the same time, they both recognize that Daniel's prophecies are fulfilled in Christ—whether he fulfilled them in the past or will fulfill them in the future. In either case, we can look forward to the day when Christ will return and reveal to us exactly how these prophecies foretold his life.

Need to Know
- The book of Daniel is made up of stories from Daniel's life as a Jewish exile in Persia and Daniel's prophetic visions.
- Daniel's visions included four beasts (chapter 7), a ram and a goat (chapter 8), a prayer with an angelic response (chapter 9), and what is considered a vision of the end times (chapters 10–12).

Think About It
- No matter which interpretation of Daniel's seventy weeks is true, how is Jesus your Messiah, your champion, your Savior today?
- In what ways do you find it difficult to deal with someone who has a very different view of the end times than you do?

Day 32

And I saw when the Lamb opened one of the seals, and I heard,
as it were the noise of thunder, one of the four beasts saying,
Come and see. And I saw, and behold a white horse:
and he that sat on him had a bow; and a crown was given unto
him: and he went forth conquering, and to conquer.
And when he had opened the second seal,
I heard the second beast say, Come and see.
And there went out another horse that was red:
and power was given to him that sat thereon to take peace
from the earth, and that they should kill one another:
and there was given unto him a great sword.
And when he had opened the third seal,
I heard the third beast say, Come and see.
And I beheld, and lo a black horse;
and he that sat on him had a pair of balances in his hand.
And I heard a voice in the midst of the four beasts say,
A measure of wheat for a penny, and three measures
of barley for a penny; and see thou hurt not the oil and the wine.
And when he had opened the fourth seal,
I heard the voice of the fourth beast say, Come and see.
And I looked, and behold a pale horse:
and his name that sat on him was Death,
and Hell followed with him.
And power was given unto them over the fourth part of the earth,
to kill with sword, and with hunger, and with death,
and with the beasts of the earth.

REVELATION 6:1–8

The Four Horsemen of the Apocalypse

In Revelation 6, John describes four horsemen as introducing God's judgment on the world. The first rides a white horse; the second, a fiery red horse; the third, a black horse; and the fourth, a pale horse. Each one has a mission related to the Lamb's breaking of the first four seals of judgment (Revelation 6:1–8).

Opening the first seal releases a rider with a bow on a white horse (Revelation 6:2). This is the only rider who doesn't cause some kind of a catastrophe on the earth. He merely rides out to win battles. There is much debate over who or what this horseman represents. Some commentators have suggested this horseman symbolizes the proclamation of the Good News of Christ, while others see him as representing the rise of false Christs. The color of the horse seems to point to the Good News interpretation, for Jesus is closely associated with the color white in Revelation (Revelation 1:14; 7:14; 14:14; 19:11). On the other hand, the fact that this white horse and rider precede four other horsemen who wreak havoc on the earth suggests that the white horseman might represent the rise of false Christs.

Need to Know
- The color white is used throughout Scripture to represent purity and holiness. "Though your sins be as scarlet, they shall be as white as snow" (Isaiah 1:18).
- In his discourse on the end times, Jesus talked about false Christs. He warned his followers to be on their guard even against those who could perform miracles (see Mark 13:22–23).

Think About It
- What Christian beliefs are you aware of upon which there are many differing interpretations?
- How do you see Jesus as a victory-winner in your life?

Table: Fast Facts on the Seven Seals

Seal	Description	Possible Meaning	Reference
First Seal: The White Horse	The rider wears a crown and carries a bow. He marches out to seek victory.	Some scholars believe the white horse stands for an outbreak of violence. Others believe it might actually represent the spread of the Good News.	Revelation 6:1–2
Second Seal: The Red Horse	The rider is given a large sword and has the power and authority to make war.	The red horse symbolizes a judgment of warfare, accompanied by other disasters.	Revelation 6:3–4
Third Seal: The Black Horse	The rider holds a pair of scales. A shout from heaven announces the lack of food and wine.	The black horse symbolizes a terrible famine.	Revelation 6:5–6
The Fourth Seal: The Pale Horse	The rider's name is Death, and its cohort is Hell. They put to death a quarter of the world's population.	The pale horse is death in its various brutal forms.	Revelation 6:7–8

Seal	Description	Possible Meaning	Reference
The Fifth Seal: The Souls Under the Altar	Under the altar are the souls of those who had been martyred for proclaiming God's word.	The events of the fifth seal, unlike the previous four, take place in the realm of the spirit. The breaking of the seal announces God's determination to judge those who persecuted believers.	Revelation 6:9–11
The Sixth Seal: The Great Earthquake	The earth is overwhelmed with natural calamities. People flee to escape God's wrath.	The earthquake reveals the wrath of the lamb, whose anger cannot be withstood. People cry out for the mountains to crush them rather than have to face God.	Revelation 6:12–17
The Seventh Seal: Silence in Heaven	The opening of the seal begins with a period of silence in heaven.	The seventh seal begins the final cycle of judgments that lead up to final battle between Christ and his enemies.	Revelation 8:1

Day 33

And when he had opened the second seal,
I heard the second beast say,
Come and see.
And there went out another horse that was red:
and power was given to him that sat
thereon to take peace from the earth,
and that they should kill one another:
and there was given unto him a great sword.
And when he had opened the third seal,
I heard the third beast say,
Come and see.
And I beheld, and lo a black horse;
and he that sat on him had a pair of balances in his hand.
And I heard a voice in the midst of the four beasts say,
A measure of wheat for a penny, and three measures of barley
for a penny; and see thou hurt not the oil and the wine.
And when he had opened the fourth seal,
I heard the voice of the fourth beast say,
Come and see.
And I looked, and behold a pale horse:
and his name that sat on him was Death,
and Hell followed with him.
And power was given unto them over the fourth part of the earth,
to kill with sword, and with hunger,
and with death, and with the beasts of the earth.
REVELATION 6:3–8

Agents of Judgment

At the breaking of the second seal, the rider of a red horse is given a large sword to provoke warfare and slaughter on the earth (Revelation 6:3–4).

The third seal unleashes a black horse whose rider holds a scale, symbolizing economic hard times and sorrow (Revelation 6:5–6, 12). A voice declares that the cost for barley and wheat are twelve to fifteen times the normal price, suggesting inflation and famine. But this famine is not extreme since other staples like olive oil and wine are not affected.

The fourth seal unleashes a pale horse, ridden by "Death," who is given power to kill a quarter of the earth's population through war, famine, plagues, and wild animals (Revelation 6:7–8). The horse's pale color suggests fear as well as impending death. "Hell" follows this horse on foot, grimly devouring the dead.

Need to Know
- A sword is used throughout the Bible as a symbol for and tool of war. It was the first weapon of offense mentioned. A sword guarded the Garden of Eden after Adam and Eve were sent away.
- Scales were a symbol of equality and judgment. While used in commerce to weigh goods, they were also mentioned by Ezekiel, Daniel, and others as a way to measure a person's integrity.

Think About It
- What are the images or symbols our culture would choose today to denote war and death?
- What elements of your relationship with God allow you to be free of the fears associated with famine, war, and death?

Day 34

For we know that the whole creation groaneth and travaileth
in pain together until now. And not only they, but ourselves also,
which have the firstfruits of the Spirit, even we ourselves groan within
ourselves, waiting for the adoption, to wit, the redemption of our body.
For we are saved by hope: but hope that is seen is not hope:
for what a man seeth, why doth he yet hope for?
ROMANS 8:22–24

And I wept much, because no man was found
worthy to open and to read the book,
neither to look thereon.
REVELATION 5:4

And when he had taken the book, the four beasts
and four and twenty elders fell down before the Lamb,
having every one of them harps, and golden vials full of odours,
which are the prayers of saints. And they sung a new song, saying,
Thou art worthy to take the book, and to open the seals thereof:
for thou wast slain, and hast redeemed us to God by thy blood out of
every kindred, and tongue, and people, and nation; And hast made us
unto our God kings and priests: and we shall reign on the earth.
REVELATION 5:8–10

The Meaning of the Horsemen

What is the meaning of these horsemen? Why does the Lamb break the seals? To answer these questions, we need to look at the broader context of this vision in Revelation.

The four horsemen are part of a vision that describes the breaking of seven seals on a bound scroll (Revelation 5). Many scholars believe that this scroll represents God's plan for history. Amillennialists interpret the scroll as God's redemptive plan for history, while premillennialists interpret it as God's plan for the final days before Jesus' second coming (Daniel 12:1–4). No wonder John weeps when no one is able to open the scroll (Revelation 5:4). If the scroll remains bound, evil will continue unabated and there will be no future for God's people. But the slain Lamb appears, and the heavenly hosts sing that he is worthy to open the scroll because he has "redeemed us to God by [his] blood" (Revelation 5:9). As a result of Christ's redemption, believers will reign with Christ on earth (Revelation 5:8–10).

Need to Know
- Jesus' role as the Lamb hearkens back to the earliest Jewish traditions of sacrificial lambs, most specifically the Passover Lamb. In Egypt, the blood of an innocent lamb was placed on the doorposts of Hebrew homes, and thus the angel of death was kept from taking the firstborn of the household (Exodus 12:21–23).
- When the Lamb, Jesus, opens the scroll, even though the immediate consequence is havoc, it is a fulfillment of the promise woven throughout the New Testament of our redemption and adoption into God's family (Romans 8:22–24).

Think About It
- What does it mean to you that you will "reign on the earth" with Christ?
- Jesus gave his life so that you could be adopted as a child of God. In what ways do you express your gratitude for that?

Day 35

And Jesus answered and said unto them,
Take heed that no man deceive you.
For many shall come in my name, saying,
I am Christ; and shall deceive many.
And ye shall hear of wars and rumours of wars:
see that ye be not troubled: for all these things must come to pass,
but the end is not yet. For nation shall rise against nation,
and kingdom against kingdom: and there shall be famines,
and pestilences, and earthquakes, in divers places.
All these are the beginning of sorrows.
MATTHEW 24:4–8

And Jesus answering them began to say,
Take heed lest any man deceive you:
For many shall come in my name, saying,
I am Christ; and shall deceive many.
And when ye shall hear of wars and rumours of wars,
be ye not troubled: for such things must needs be;
but the end shall not be yet. For nation shall rise against nation,
and kingdom against kingdom: and there shall be earthquakes
in divers places, and there shall be famines and troubles:
these are the beginnings of sorrows.
MARK 13:5–8

And he said,
Take heed that ye be not deceived:
for many shall come in my name, saying,
I am Christ; and the time draweth near:
go ye not therefore after them.
But when ye shall hear of wars and commotions,
be not terrified: for these things must first come to pass;
but the end is not by and by.
LUKE 21:8–9

THE SCROLL AND ITS SEVEN SEALS

What is the relationship between the seals and the content of the scroll (see Revelation 6)? To open an ancient scroll, a person had to break every wax seal. Some commentators believe that the seals described in Revelation are predicting what will occur before the scroll is opened— that is, before the end of the world. Note the striking similarities between Jesus' description of the "beginning pains" of the end times and the breaking of these four seals. Jesus declared that false Christs, wars, famines, plagues, and persecutions would precede his Second Coming (Matthew 24:4–8; Mark 13:5–13; Luke 21:8–19), just as is described in the vision of the seals in Revelation.

Need to Know
- Just like safety seals appear today on foods and medicines ("Do not open if seal is broken") or documents that are notarized, ancient scrolls were sealed with wax or clay. The seals were often stamped with the sender's seal, usually kept as a ring on his finger or around his neck. These ancient seals functioned in the same way as their modern counterparts, both for protection and validation of the contents.
- In the ancient world, a pestilence (a contagious epidemic disease) was seen as an act of judgment from God rather than a natural phenomenon or random event.

Think About It
- How do you make sense of God's plan when everything is going wrong all around?
- What recent headlines seem to be a part of the "beginning of sorrows" that Jesus described in Mark?

Day 36

Be not overcome of evil, but overcome evil with good.
ROMANS 12:21

*I write unto you, fathers, because ye have known him
that is from the beginning. I write unto you, young men,
because ye have overcome the wicked one.
I write unto you, little children, because ye have known the Father.
I have written unto you, fathers, because ye have known him
that is from the beginning. I have written unto you,
young men, because ye are strong,
and the word of God abideth in you,
and ye have overcome the wicked one.*
1 JOHN 2:13–14

*These shall make war with the Lamb,
and the Lamb shall overcome them: for he is Lord of lords,
and King of kings: and they that are with him are called,
and chosen, and faithful.*
REVELATION 17:14

The Meaning of the Breaking of the Seals

Why does Christ break the scroll's seals and permit such devastation? Keep in mind that the Revelation was written for Christians who were being persecuted. In breaking these seals, Christ isn't ordering devastation and destruction. Such evil already exists in this world. Rather, the description of Christ breaking the seals demonstrates his lordship over human history—even the evil that occurs in history. This vision assures believers that despite present appearances, Christ is unfolding a future in which he will triumph over every enemy (Revelation 17:14). Believers can have this confidence because Jesus Christ reigns.

Need to Know
- Persecution for first-century Christianity began almost as soon as the movement was recognized. Jesus' life was filled with persecution. After his ascension back to heaven, his followers were persecuted by the Jews for perpetuating the gospel story. When the Christians then refused to worship Caesar, they became enemies of the state.
- From the first conflict between God and Adam and Eve, and between Cain and Abel, evil has been a part of our world. Many words are used to denote evil in biblical texts, most of them containing some element of destruction, disaster, calamity, wickedness, and downfall.

Think About It
- What specific enemies or evils of this world do you look forward to Jesus triumphing over?
- In the midst of the troubles in the world and the coming greater troubles, what signs of God's redemption and sovereignty do you see?

Day 37

But as the days of Noe were,
so shall also the coming of the Son of man be.
For as in the days that were before the flood they were
eating and drinking, marrying and giving in marriage,
until the day that Noe entered into the ark,
And knew not until the flood came, and took them all away;
so shall also the coming of the Son of man be.
Then shall two be in the field; the one shall be taken,
and the other left. Two women shall be grinding at the mill; the one shall
be taken, and the other left. Watch therefore: for ye know not what hour
your Lord doth come. But know this, that if the goodman of the house
had known in what watch the thief would come, he would have watched,
and would not have suffered his house to be broken up.
Therefore be ye also ready:
for in such an hour as ye think not the Son of man cometh.
MATTHEW 24:37–44

For the Lord himself shall descend from heaven with a shout,
with the voice of the archangel, and with the trump of God:
and the dead in Christ shall rise first:
Then we which are alive and remain shall be caught up together
with them in the clouds, to meet the Lord in the air:
and so shall we ever be with the Lord.
Wherefore comfort one another with these words.
1 THESSALONIANS 4:16–18

THE RAPTURE

"Two women shall be grinding at a mill; the one shall be taken, and the other left" (Matthew 24:41). Jesus' description of the day he returns has sparked the imaginations of many. What would it be like if half of a town's population suddenly disappeared? Would cars spin out of control, as those bumper stickers suggest: "WARNING: In case of rapture this vehicle will be unattended"?

The term *rapture,* meaning "to seize" or "to carry away," is an integral part of Paul's description of Christ's return. At this event, believers are literally pulled up to meet Christ in the air (1 Thessalonians 4:16–18). While most Christians believe in a future rapture event, there are obviously a variety of views regarding its nature and timing.

Need to Know
- The Rapture will be, among other things, a mass resurrection. Paul said, "the dead in Christ shall rise first." There were a few resurrections in Scripture before the resurrection of Jesus. Through God's power, the prophet Elisha raised a boy from the dead (2 Kings 4). Jesus raised people from the dead, perhaps the most famous being Lazarus: "Lazarus, come forth!" (John 11).
- From the beginning, death has been the enemy. Eve's conversation with the serpent was about death ("Ye shall not surely die. . ."). Jesus' resurrection was a victory over death. While the end times, including the Rapture, can be mysterious and even scary, it is about life over death.

Think About It
- What do you or others you know fear about the Rapture?
- If you were given the job of fashioning a new end-times bumper sticker, what would it say?

DAY 38

And I will give power unto my two witnesses,
and they shall prophesy a thousand two hundred and threescore days,
clothed in sackcloth. These are the two olive trees,
and the two candlesticks standing before the God of the earth.
And if any man will hurt them, fire proceedeth out of their mouth,
and devoureth their enemies: and if any man will hurt them,
he must in this manner be killed. These have power to shut heaven,
that it rain not in the days of their prophecy:
and have power over waters to turn them to blood,
and to smite the earth with all plagues, as often as they will.
And when they shall have finished their testimony,
the beast that ascendeth out of the bottomless pit shall make war
against them, and shall overcome them, and kill them.
And their dead bodies shall lie in the street of the great city,
which spiritually is called Sodom and Egypt,
where also our Lord was crucified.
And they of the people and kindreds and tongues
and nations shall see their dead bodies three days and an half,
and shall not suffer their dead bodies to be put in graves.
And they that dwell upon the earth shall rejoice over them,
and make merry, and shall send gifts one to another;
because these two prophets tormented them that dwelt on the earth.
And after three days and an half the Spirit of life from God
entered into them, and they stood upon their feet;
and great fear fell upon them which saw them.
REVELATION 11:3–11

Two Witnesses in Jerusalem

In the midst of the Tribulation, a period of unprecedented evil and persecution, two voices will shout out a message of hope. Revelation 11:3–13 tells us that two witnesses will preach God's word in Jerusalem and throughout the world for 1,260 days. Anyone who tries to harm these messengers during that time will be destroyed. These two witnesses for God will possess supernatural powers—the ability to stop rain from falling, to turn water into blood, and to cause plagues.

After three and a half years, the witnesses will be killed by the beast, the antichrist. For three and a half days, their dead bodies will lie in the street for the whole world to see—perhaps this spectacle will be viewed via satellite television. In any case, the whole world will celebrate because they won't have to listen to the two witnesses anymore. The celebration will be short-lived, though. After their bodies have been left in the streets for three and a half days, the witnesses will be brought back to life and will ascend to heaven. Their resurrection will frighten people and cause many to turn to Christ.

Need to Know
- There has been much speculation as to the identity of the two witnesses. Some believe that they will be Enoch and Elijah, both Old Testament ancients who were taken to heaven without dying. Others believe they will be Moses and Elijah, who did similar miracles to those described in Revelation 11. Still others believe the two witnesses are just symbols of the church.
- John wrote that the witnesses would be dressed in sackcloth. This was a symbol of mourning. Sackcloth was usually coarse and dark. It was often worn by prophets who grieved over the sins of their people or warned them of coming doom.

Think About It
- What grieves you most about the current state of the church?
- If you were one of the last witnesses on earth, what would you say?

Day 39

For there shall arise false Christs, and false prophets,
and shall shew great signs and wonders;
insomuch that, if it were possible,
they shall deceive the very elect.
MATTHEW 24:24

And I beheld another beast coming up out of the earth;
and he had two horns like a lamb, and he spake as a dragon.
And he exerciseth all the power of the first beast before him,
and causeth the earth and them which dwell therein to worship the first
beast, whose deadly wound was healed. And he doeth great wonders,
so that he maketh fire come down from heaven on the earth in the sight
of men, And deceiveth them that dwell on the earth by the means of those
miracles which he had power to do in the sight of the beast; saying to
them that dwell on the earth, that they should make an image to the
beast, which had the wound by a sword, and did live.
REVELATION 13:11–14

FALSE PROPHETS

"For there shall arise false Christs, and false prophets." Jesus' words in Matthew 24:24 serve as a warning to believers of every generation. They will be especially applicable to the people living during the end times. Revelation 13:11–17 describes a "second beast," one who will persuade the world to follow the first beast, the antichrist (Revelation 13:1–10). This second beast, also known as the false prophet, will use supernatural tricks and miracles—such as calling down fire from heaven and bringing a statue to life—to deceive people into worshiping the antichrist. Those who don't evaluate this false prophet's teaching against the truth of God's Word, those who don't have the courage to reject this prophet, will be caught under his spell.

Need to Know
- Some believe that this second beast is an actual individual, but others believe it will be a movement or power that takes worldwide control.
- This second beast completes what some people refer to as the "unholy trinity," made up of Satan, the antichrist, and the prophet—counterparts to the Father, Son, and Holy Spirit.

Think About It
- What vulnerabilities do you see around you that sets up our society to be easily deceived by false prophets?
- What can you do today to ensure that you know the truth well enough not to be deceived by false teachers?

DAY 40

And Jesus came and spake unto them, saying,
All power is given unto me in heaven and in earth.
Go ye therefore, and teach all nations,
baptizing them in the name of the Father,
and of the Son, and of the Holy Ghost:
Teaching them to observe all things whatsoever
I have commanded you: and, lo,
I am with you alway, even unto the end of the world. Amen.
MATTHEW 28:18–20

For the word of God is quick, and powerful,
and sharper than any twoedged sword,
piercing even to the dividing asunder of soul and spirit,
and of the joints and marrow, and is a discerner of the thoughts
and intents of the heart.
HEBREWS 4:12

And he had in his right hand seven stars:
and out of his mouth went a sharp twoedged sword:
and his countenance was as the sun shineth in his strength.
REVELATION 1:16

Postmillennial View

Postmillennialists believe that Christ is currently leading his church to victory over all its enemies through the renewing power of God's Word (Matthew 28:18–20). Evangelists and Christians who try to spread the Good News of Christ will always face obstacles. Yet postmillennialists don't believe that wickedness and persecution will significantly increase as the world draws to a close.

Postmillennialists insist that the church today is transforming society gradually in the same way that yeast permeates bread (Matthew 13:33). They believe Armageddon represents Christ's victory over evil forces throughout church history. They point out that Scripture describes the Lamb as conquering with the sword of his mouth—in other words, Jesus conquers his enemies spiritually, through the preaching of God's Word (Hebrews 4:12; Revelation 19:11–21). In this way, God will triumph over all opposition and establish a period of spiritual prosperity: the millennial kingdom.

Need to Know
- The Psalms as well as many New Testament verses tell about the benefits of God's Word. The Scriptures equip us, renew us, restore us, feed us, and more.
- At the beginning of Revelation, John gave messages to seven churches. The image he described there of Jesus, the Son of man, included a two-edged sword coming out of his mouth (Revelation 1:16). This image fits perfectly with the description in Hebrews 4:12 of God's word being "sharper than any twoedged sword."

Think About It
- How has God transformed you through his Word?
- How do you see the world becoming a better place (or having the potential of it) through God's Word?

Timeline for the

Jesus is currently
conquering his enemies.
(Rev. 19:11)

Jesus'
Resurrection

Church Age   Millennium

A.D. **70** —
Jerusalem
Destroyed

Church Age

- Church gradually brings
  about the millennium
  by preaching the Good
  News.

- Prophecies concerning
  the tribulation were
  fulfilled in A.D. 70, when
  the Romans destroyed
  Jerusalem. No future
  tribulation.

Bottomless Pit

Satan is thrown in
the bottomless pit
at the end of the
Church Age.

The Millennium

- Jesus reigns during
  the millennium in
  a spiritual sense.

- The whole world
  worships Jesus.

- The culture
  becomes
  "Christian."

- No war.

Postmillennial View

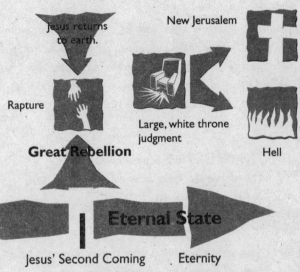

Jesus returns to earth.

New Jerusalem

Rapture

Large, white throne judgment

Hell

Great Rebellion

Eternal State

Jesus' Second Coming

- Jesus returns to defeat Satan's Great Rebellion.
- Believers meet Jesus in midair.
- All are raised from the dead to be judged by Christ.

Eternity

- Believers go to the New Jerusalem.
- Unbelievers go to hell.

Day 41

There hath no temptation taken you but such as is common to man:
but God is faithful, who will not suffer you to be tempted
above that ye are able; but will with the temptation also
make a way to escape, that ye may be able to bear it.
1 CORINTHIANS 10:13

For God hath not appointed us to wrath,
but to obtain salvation by our Lord Jesus Christ,
1 THESSALONIANS 5:9

Even him, whose coming is after the working of Satan
with all power and signs and lying wonders,
And with all deceivableness of unrighteousness in them that perish;
because they received not the love of the truth, that they might be saved.
And for this cause God shall send them strong delusion,
that they should believe a lie:
That they all might be damned who believed not the truth,
but had pleasure in unrighteousness.
2 THESSALONIANS 2:9–12

Amillennial and Historic Premillennial View

Both amillennialists and historic premillennialists believe evil and destruction will increase tremendously in the last days. They point out that Jesus predicted a future of persecution and catastrophe. This time of tribulation will culminate in the antichrist, who will proclaim himself as a god, lead a worldwide rebellion against the true God, and persecute Christians (Matthew 24:15–22; 2 Thessalonians 2:3–12). Both these views insist that Christians will be present on earth during this awful period of tribulation since Scripture never promises their escape. However, God *does* promise spiritual protection for his people during times of persecution (1 Corinthians 10:13; 1 Thessalonians 1:10; 5:9).

Both amillennialists and historic premillennialists believe that the vision of Armageddon in Revelation figuratively portrays the final rebellion against God. As a result, they place more attention on the Second Coming than on the actual battle itself.

Need to Know
- There are many parts of the Bible over which scholars and theologians disagree about whether the narrative is symbolic or whether the events actually did (or will) occur. Still, there are many applications and encouragements to be found in these very Scriptures no matter which way a person leans on the issue.
- Remember that the antichrist is one of the three in the unholy trinity of Satan, the antichrist, and the false prophet.

Think About It
- If Christians do remain on earth through the Tribulation, how can you and others be ready?
- What are you facing in this season of life that will prepare you for tribulations and persecutions?

DAY 42

And the ten horns out of this kingdom
are ten kings that shall arise:
and another shall rise after them;
and he shall be diverse from the first,
and he shall subdue three kings.
And he shall speak great words against the most High,
and shall wear out the saints of the most High,
and think to change times and laws:
and they shall be given into his hand
until a time and times and the dividing of time.
DANIEL 7:24–25

And he gathered them together into a place
called in the Hebrew tongue Armageddon.
REVELATION 16:16

And I saw the beast, and the kings of the earth,
and their armies, gathered together to make war
against him that sat on the horse, and against his army.
And the beast was taken, and with him
the false prophet that wrought miracles before him,
with which he deceived them that had received the mark of the beast,
and them that worshipped his image.
These both were cast alive into a lake of fire burning with brimstone.
And the remnant were slain with the sword of him
that sat upon the horse, which sword proceeded out of his mouth:
and all the fowls were filled with their flesh.
REVELATION 19:19–21

DISPENSATIONAL PREMILLENNIAL VIEW

Dispensational premillennialists have developed a detailed scenario for what they see as the battle of Armageddon. They believe the future tribulation will not begin until after the Rapture—that time when all believers, living and dead, meet the Lord in midair and return to heaven with him. Dispensationalists believe that God will use the Tribulation to bring Israel back to himself.

During the Tribulation, the antichrist emerges as the leader of the restored Roman Empire. At first the antichrist befriends Israel. But after three and a half years, he begins a horrible persecution of the Jews (Daniel 7:8, 20–27; 9:24–27; Matthew 24:15–22). Because of this, Israel begins to return to God. At the height of his persecution of God's people, the antichrist's own worldwide power base begins to crumble. The battle of Armageddon begins when the king of the north and the king of the south converge on Israel to attack the antichrist and his troops. After these armies are defeated, the kings of the east invade Israel, resulting in the final campaign of Armageddon (Revelation 16:16). Then at the last hour, Christ miraculously and decisively intervenes in this horrific battle. At the battlefield of Armageddon, he demonstrates his power and destroys all remaining foes (Revelation 19:19–21).

Need to Know
- The kings involved in Armageddon (and pre-Armageddon) are probably the national leaders who join in alliance with the antichrist.
- It is after Christ's victory at Armageddon that the lake of fire comes into play. It is the final destination of all that is evil.

Think About It
- What typifies evil in your culture?
- What does Christ's definitive victory over all evil offer you today as you battle with evil in your world?

Timeline for the

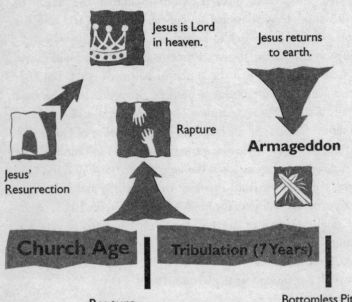

Jesus is Lord in heaven.

Jesus returns to earth.

Rapture

Armageddon

Jesus' Resurrection

Church Age

Tribulation (7 Years)

Rapture

- Before the tribulation, Jesus raises dead believers and takes living believers to heaven.
- Believers are judged.

Bottomless Pit

Christ's Second Coming

- Christ defeats the antichrist at Armageddon.
- Christ throws Satan in the bottomless pit.
- Tribulation martyrs are raised from the dead

Dispensational Premillennial View

New Jerusalem

Large, white throne
judgment

Hell

Millennium (1,000 Years)

Eternal State

The Millennium

- Jesus physically rules on earth for 1,000 years.

End of the Millennium

- Unbelievers are raised from the dead to be judged.

Eternity

- Believers go to the New Jerusalem.
- Unbelievers go to hell.

Day 43

And Jesus knew their thoughts, and said unto them,
Every kingdom divided against itself is brought to desolation;
and every city or house divided against itself shall not stand:
And if Satan cast out Satan, he is divided against himself;
how shall then his kingdom stand? And if I by Beelzebub cast out devils,
by whom do your children cast them out?
therefore they shall be your judges.
But if I cast out devils by the Spirit of God,
then the kingdom of God is come unto you.
Or else how can one enter into a strong man's house,
and spoil his goods, except he first bind the strong man?
and then he will spoil his house.
MATTHEW 12:25–29

I am he that liveth, and was dead; and, behold,
I am alive for evermore, Amen;
and have the keys of hell and of death.
REVELATION 1:18

And God shall wipe away all tears from their eyes;
and there shall be no more death, neither sorrow, nor crying,
neither shall there be any more pain:
for the former things are passed away.
REVELATION 21:4

Evil Will Be Conquered

While interpretations of the closing events of the Tribulation and of Armageddon differ sharply, all believers agree that Jesus has already defeated both Satan and death itself (Matthew 12:25–29; Revelation 1:18). Ultimately, evil won't prevail. One way or another, Christ will decisively demonstrate his power over Satan and his evil forces. So we don't have to concentrate on the hardships of the Tribulation or the suffering at Armageddon, we can look forward to a new age in which Christ "will wipe away all tears" from our eyes and evil will be no more (Revelation 21:4).

Need to Know
- Christ's ultimate victory over evil was first foretold by God to the serpent that deceived Eve. He promised that one would come that would bruise that serpent's head (Genesis 3:14). It is at the end of Armageddon that Jesus makes good on that promise.
- The force of evil has always been a force of destruction. God is the source of life and God's path leads to life. Jesus himself claimed to be the way, the truth, and the life. A victory over evil is victory over death itself.

Think About It
- Who do you see as the victims of evil in the world around you?
- What do you see as your role in the battle against evil?

Day 44

For thou hast said in thine heart,
I will ascend into heaven,
I will exalt my throne above the stars of God:
I will sit also upon the mount of the congregation,
in the sides of the north:
I will ascend above the heights of the clouds;
I will be like the most High.

ISAIAH 14:13–14

And the angels which kept not their first estate,
but left their own habitation, he hath reserved in everlasting chains
under darkness unto the judgment of the great day.

JUDE 1:6

And the great dragon was cast out,
that old serpent, called the Devil,
and Satan, which deceiveth the whole world:
he was cast out into the earth,
and his angels were cast out with him.

REVELATION 12:9

Satan's War with God

According to Genesis 1–2, God created human beings for relationship with himself and placed them in a paradise called the Garden of Eden. Satan, disguised as a serpent, disrupted God's plan by leading Adam and Eve into disobedience (Genesis 3:13–15; Revelation 12:9). So people are enslaved to a power greater than they are—namely, Satan, the prince of evil (Matthew 12:22–32; 1 John 5:19).

Satan was originally an angel created for God's glory. But Satan arrogantly rebelled, desiring to be like God, and was thrown from heaven (Jude 1:6). Satan's flamboyant pride is reflected in the words of the prophets Ezekiel and Isaiah to the kings of Babylon: "Thus saith the Lord God; Thou sealest up the sum, full of wisdom, and perfect in beauty. . . . Thine heart was lifted up because of thy beauty, thou hast corrupted thy wisdom by reason of thy brightness: I will cast thee to the ground" (Ezekiel 28:12, 17). "For thou hast said in thine heart, I will ascend into heaven, I will exalt my throne above the stars of God: I will sit also upon the mount of the congregation, in the sides of the north: I will ascend above the heights of the clouds; I will be like the most High" (Isaiah 14:13–14).

Need to Know
- The name *Satan* comes from a Hebrew word that means "accuser" (see Revelation 12:10). In the Old Testament Satan is portrayed as the one who tries to sit as judge on God. The name *Devil* is a Greek translation of the same name.
- In John's Gospel he referred to Satan (quoting Jesus) as the "prince of this world" (John 12:31). While it is true that Satan has some dominion over our world, God is still sovereign and will overcome in the end.

Think About It
- Do you see the will of Satan in any part of the world around you?
- What are your greatest weapons to stand against Satan and his forces?

Table: Satan's Aliases

Satan's Title	Reference
Accuser of Jesus' brothers and sisters	Revelation 12:10
Abaddon (meaning "destroyer")	Revelation 9:11
Angel of light	2 Corinthians 11:14–15
Adversary	1 Peter 5:8
Beelzebub, the prince/ruler of demons	Matthew 12:24
Deceiver	Revelation 20:10
Devil	Revelation 12:9
Enemy	Matthew 13:39
Wicked one	Matthew 13:38
Father of lies and a liar	Genesis 3:4–5; John 8:44
Leviathan, the serpent	Isaiah 27:1
Lucifer, son of the morning	Isaiah 14:12
Murderer	John 8:4
One with the power of death	Hebrews 2:14
Prince of this world	John 12:31; 14:30; 16:11
A roaring lion	1 Peter 5:8
Ruler of the darkness of this world	Ephesians 6:12
Satan	Revelation 12:9
Serpent	Revelation 12:9
Spirit working in those who refuse to obey God	Ephesians 2:2
Tempter	1 Thessalonians 3:5

Day 45

Ye are of your father the devil,
and the lusts of your father ye will do.
He was a murderer from the beginning,
and abode not in the truth,
because there is no truth in him.
When he speaketh a lie, he speaketh of his own:
for he is a liar, and the father of it.
JOHN 8:44

And they worshipped the dragon which gave power unto the beast:
and they worshipped the beast, saying,
Who is like unto the beast? who is able to make war with him?
And there was given unto him a mouth speaking great things
and blasphemies; and power was given unto him
to continue forty and two months.
And he opened his mouth in blasphemy against God,
to blaspheme his name, and his tabernacle,
and them that dwell in heaven.
And it was given unto him to make war with the saints,
and to overcome them: and power was given him over all kindreds,
and tongues, and nations.
And all that dwell upon the earth shall worship him,
whose names are not written in the book of life of the Lamb
slain from the foundation of the world.
REVELATION 13:4–8

Satan's Wicked Work

When Adam and Eve rebelled, they were hoping they could become like God and free themselves from God. But in reality, they allowed the entire human race to be enslaved to Satan. Scripture repeatedly describes Satan as the "ruler" or "god of this world" (John 14:30; 2 Corinthians 4:4). His rule pervades every area of this world. Oppressive and unjust political structures reveal Satan's reign (Revelation 12:13; 13:4–8; 18:1–20). Even the curse of death and sickness that God pronounced in Eden reflects Satan's work (Mark 5:1–15; John 8:44).

Need to Know
- Satan's claim to Eve in the Garden was that God had lied to her. The serpent said that Eve wouldn't die if she ate the fruit, as God had said. Instead, she would become like God. Satan's role from the beginning was to undermine the truth of who God is and what he says.
- Jesus was once accused of working through the power of Satan. It was in response to that accusation that Jesus gave an often-quoted reply: "a house divided against itself shall not stand" (Luke 11:17). This reply pointed out to his accusers their lack of logic. The very miracle Jesus had performed was the casting out of demons. Why would he have done that under the power of Satan?

Think About It
- Can you spot areas in your life where God's truth has been undermined?
- How would you define the work of Satan in this modern world?

Day 46

*And I will put enmity between thee and the woman,
and between thy seed and her seed; it shall bruise thy head,
and thou shalt bruise his heel.*
GENESIS 3:15

*And he said unto them,
I beheld Satan as lightning fall from heaven.
Behold, I give unto you power to tread on serpents and scorpions,
and over all the power of the enemy:
and nothing shall by any means hurt you.*
LUKE 10:18–19

*Now is the judgment of this world:
now shall the prince of this world be cast out.
And I, if I be lifted up from the earth,
will draw all men unto me.
This he said, signifying what death he should die.*
JOHN 12:31–33

Satan's Struggle with God

After Adam and Eve's sin in the Garden of Eden, God promised that he would destroy Satan and his demons and reestablish his own kingdom. Speaking to the serpent, God said, "And I will put enmity between thee and the woman, and between thy seed and her seed; it shall bruise thy head, and thou shalt bruise his heel" (Genesis 3:15). The offspring who ultimately crushes Satan's head is God's promised Messiah, Jesus Christ.

When Jesus demonstrated his power over Satan's realm through his miracles and exorcisms, he was, in a sense, binding the "strong man" of this world (Matthew 12:28–29). Hearing of his disciples' success on their first mission to spread his word, Jesus said, "I beheld Satan as lightning fall from heaven. Behold, I give unto you power. . .over all the power of the enemy" (Luke 10:18–19).

Jesus' sacrificial death on the cross and his resurrection sealed his victory over Satan. Christ disarmed the evil powers and authorities (Colossians 2:15; John 12:31; 16:11).

Need to Know
- Christ's death on the cross appeared to be a defeat, yet it was the moment of greatest victory. It was the connecting point between God's promise in the Garden and Jesus' eventual victory at Armageddon.
- During Jesus' time on earth, Satan's demons recognized him as the Son of God long before Jesus' fellow Israelites did. The demons recognized Jesus' authority. When he was casting the demons out of Legion, they spoke up to negotiate their transfer into the swine rather than being sent away (Mark 5:1–13).

Think About It
- What does it mean to you that Jesus has given Christians authority over Satan?
- What fears, if any, do you have regarding Satan's power and influence?

DAY 47

Submit yourselves therefore to God.
Resist the devil, and he will flee from you.
JAMES 4:7

Be sober, be vigilant; because your adversary the devil,
as a roaring lion, walketh about, seeking whom he may devour:
Whom resist stedfast in the faith, knowing that the same afflictions
are accomplished in your brethren that are in the world.
But the God of all grace, who hath called us unto his eternal glory
by Christ Jesus, after that ye have suffered a while,
make you perfect, stablish, strengthen, settle you.
1 PETER 5:8–10

And there was war in heaven:
Michael and his angels fought against the dragon;
and the dragon fought and his angels,
And prevailed not; neither was their place found any more in heaven.
And the great dragon was cast out, that old serpent, called the Devil,
and Satan, which deceiveth the whole world:
he was cast out into the earth,
and his angels were cast out with him.
REVELATION 12:7–9

SATAN'S FINAL BATTLE

Revelation 12:7–9 describes a war in heaven between Satan and the archangel Michael. After Satan is defeated and ejected from heaven, his battle against God's people becomes even more ruthless (Revelation 12:12). Now in his death throes, Satan "walketh about, seeking whom he may devour" (1 Peter 5:8). Members of the first-century church understood Satan's intentions. They warned one another to resist evil (James 4:7) and even expected "to suffer a lot" (Acts 14:22; John 16:33). Believers have only experienced the first stage of Christ's victory over Satan. While Satan's final destruction is certain, we are presently waiting for Christ to "bruise Satan" and to end all evil (Romans 16:20).

Our only hope against Satan is Jesus Christ. Christ alone is more powerful than Satan. His grace, brought to us by the Holy Spirit, can put Satan on the run (Romans 8:26; 1 Peter 5:8–10). Guard yourself against Satan by keeping your eyes fixed on Jesus!

Need to Know
- Peter's description of Satan attacking as a lion is an apt one. In the wild, lions often attack the weak, sick, or struggling—those who will fall most easily.
- Paul also warned against the attacks of Satan. One of his most famous warnings is a preamble to the description of the armor of God (Ephesians 6:12).

Think About It
- What will be my most vulnerable place today, the place where evil could influence me?
- How can I, in a practical way, trust in God's power over Satan's evil?

Day 48

Therefore, behold, the days come,
that I will do judgment upon the graven images of Babylon:
and her whole land shall be confounded,
and all her slain shall fall in the midst of her.
Then the heaven and the earth, and all that is therein,
shall sing for Babylon:
for the spoilers shall come unto her from the north, saith the Lord.
As Babylon hath caused the slain of Israel to fall,
so at Babylon shall fall the slain of all the earth.
JEREMIAH 51:47–49

Standing afar off for the fear of her torment, saying,
Alas, alas, that great city Babylon,
that mighty city! for in one hour is thy judgment come.
And the merchants of the earth shall weep and mourn over her;
for no man buyeth their merchandise any more:
The merchandise of gold, and silver, and precious stones,
and of pearls, and fine linen, and purple, and silk,
and scarlet, and all thyine wood, and all manner vessels of ivory,
and all manner vessels of most precious wood, and of brass, and iron,
and marble, And cinnamon, and odours, and ointments,
and frankincense, and wine, and oil, and fine flour, and wheat,
and beasts, and sheep, and horses, and chariots, and slaves,
and souls of men. And the fruits that thy soul lusted after are departed
from thee, and all things which were dainty and goodly are departed
from thee, and thou shalt find them no more at all.
REVELATION 18:10–14

Babylon: The Notorious Prostitute

Babylon is the name given to the satanically influenced civilization that figures prominently in end-time events. Babylon is the wellspring of ungodly religion, government, and economics. From the wickedness of Babylon, the most evil ruler the world has ever known, the beast (antichrist) will emerge. In Revelation 17, an angel calls Babylon a notorious prostitute. She will tempt the rulers of every nation to blaspheme God and commit sexual sins. The beast will use Babylon's false religion to gain power. Once the beast is established, he will turn against Babylon and create his own religious system (Revelation 17:16–17). The beast will utterly demolish Babylon and all its luxuries (Revelation 18), and the merchants of the world will weep over this fallen civilization.

Need to Know
- Ancient Babylon is often mentioned in Old Testament prophecies. It was Babylon that finally overtook Judah (what remained of the nation of Israel) and carried the Jews into exile (Jeremiah 51:47–49; 2 Kings 25:21).
- From the time of ancient Israel, the spiritual unfaithfulness of the people was described in terms of adultery. That is why Babylon is described as a prostitute; the false religions of Babylon seduced God's people away.

Think About It
- What "Babylons" do you sense around you—modern influences that deliberately try to undermine the Christian faith?
- What are your own personal "Babylons" that pull and tear at your spirituality?

Day 49

And I saw an angel come down from heaven,
having the key of the bottomless pit and a great chain in his hand.
And he laid hold on the dragon, that old serpent, which is the Devil,
and Satan, and bound him a thousand years,
And cast him into the bottomless pit, and shut him up,
and set a seal upon him, that he should deceive the nations no more,
till the thousand years should be fulfilled:
and after that he must be loosed a little season.

REVELATION 20:1–3

And when the thousand years are expired,
Satan shall be loosed out of his prison,
And shall go out to deceive the nations which are
in the four quarters of the earth, Gog and Magog,
to gather them together to battle:
the number of whom is as the sand of the sea.
And they went up on the breadth of the earth,
and compassed the camp of the saints about, and the beloved city:
and fire came down from God out of heaven, and devoured them.
And the devil that deceived them was cast into the lake of fire
and brimstone, where the beast and the false prophet are,
and shall be tormented day and night for ever and ever.

REVELATION 20:7–10

THE GREAT RED DRAGON

"Great red dragon" is one of John's favorite nicknames for Satan. In Revelation 12, the apostle witnesses a war in heaven between God's angels led by Michael, and the forces of evil led by the red dragon, or serpent. After losing the battle, Satan and his angels will be thrown out of heaven to the earth. Recognizing that his time on earth is short, the serpent will use the beast (antichrist) to wage war against God's people (Revelation 13:1–2). When Jesus returns, the serpent will be overpowered and chained in the bottomless pit for "a thousand years" (Revelation 20:2). At the end of that time, he will be released briefly and allowed to wreak havoc by deceiving anyone he can into joining him in a war against God. The serpent's eternal fate will be sealed when he is thrown into the fiery lake of sulfur forever (Revelation 20:7–10).

Need to Know
- In Scripture there are often parallels between good and evil. Here Satan is referred to as a great red dragon and serpent. Moses once used a bronze serpent sculpture on a pole to grant healing to his people suffering from poisonous snakebites. In the New Testament that snake statue was referred to as a symbol of Christ's crucifixion and its healing power. Symbols can mean different things in different situations.
- The bottomless pit, the abyss, is the exact opposite of heaven. It is the seat of wickedness and destruction. It is the source of evil, just as heaven is the source of God's goodness.

Think About It
- What are the ways in which you think "red serpent" is an apt description of Satan as you have observed his work in your lifetime?
- In what ways do you now see Satan fighting against God's people?

Day 50

And the great dragon was cast out, that old serpent,
called the Devil, and Satan,
which deceiveth the whole world:
he was cast out into the earth,
and his angels were cast out with him.
REVELATION 12:9

And the fifth angel poured out his vial
upon the seat of the beast;
and his kingdom was full of darkness;
and they gnawed their tongues for pain,
And blasphemed the God of heaven
because of their pains and their sores,
and repented not of their deeds.
And the sixth angel poured out his vial
upon the great river Euphrates;
and the water thereof was dried up, that the way
of the kings of the east might be prepared.
And I saw three unclean spirits like frogs
come out of the mouth of the dragon,
and out of the mouth of the beast,
and out of the mouth of the false prophet.
For they are the spirits of devils, working miracles,
which go forth unto the kings of the earth and of the whole world,
to gather them to the battle of that great day of God Almighty.
REVELATION 16:10–14

THE RELEASE OF THE DEMONS

Demons have always made effective villains and monsters in our culture. Their supernatural abilities and evil nature have provided images and tales for countless novels, television shows, and movies. But how accurate are these portrayals? Are demons really dangerous, frightening beings?

Demons are fallen angels (Revelation 12:9). They are sinful spiritual beings who recognize Satan as their leader (Matthew 25:41; Luke 11:15). The book of Revelation highlights three evil powers who oppose God's people in the end times: Satan, in the guise of a serpent (Revelation 12:9); the beast, better known as the antichrist (Revelation 13:1–10); and the false prophet (Revelation 13:11; 16:13). Demons serve as agents of this evil trinity. They seduce people, establish the notorious kingdom of Babylon, and lead a worldwide offensive against God's people (Revelation 16:1–14).

Need to Know
- Jesus was accused of doing his work through the power of Beelzebub, the chief of demons. *Beelzebub,* literally meaning "lord of the flies," was another name for Satan.
- The English word for *demon* is derived from a Greek word that means "deity," in this case false deities. There is no specific Hebrew word for demon, but there are Old Testament references to evil spirits.

Think About It
- What is the most effective portrayal of a demon you've witnessed in modern culture?
- In what ways do you think our culture either trivializes or magnifies the work of Satan and his demons?

Day 51

For we wrestle not against flesh and blood,
but against principalities, against powers,
against the rulers of the darkness of this world,
against spiritual wickedness in high places.

Ephesians 6:12

And they worshipped the dragon
which gave power unto the beast:
and they worshipped the beast, saying,
Who is like unto the beast? who is able to make war with him?
And there was given unto him a mouth speaking
great things and blasphemies; and power was given
unto him to continue forty and two months.
And he opened his mouth in blasphemy against God,
to blaspheme his name, and his tabernacle,
and them that dwell in heaven.
And it was given unto him to make war with the saints,
and to overcome them:
and power was given him over all kindreds,
and tongues, and nations.
And all that dwell upon the earth shall worship him,
whose names are not written in the book of
life of the Lamb slain from the foundation of the world.
If any man have an ear, let him hear.
He that leadeth into captivity shall go into captivity:
he that killeth with the sword must be killed with the sword.
Here is the patience and the faith of the saints.
And I beheld another beast coming up out of the earth;
and he had two horns like a lamb, and he spake as a dragon.
And he exerciseth all the power of the first beast before him,

*and causeth the earth and them which dwell therein
to worship the first beast, whose deadly wound was healed.
And he doeth great wonders, so that he maketh fire
come down from heaven on the earth in the sight of men,
And deceiveth them that dwell on the earth by the means of those
miracles which he had power to do in the sight of the beast;
saying to them that dwell on the earth,
that they should make an image to the beast,
which had the wound by a sword, and did live.
And he had power to give life unto the image of the beast,
that the image of the beast should both speak,
and cause that as many as would not worship
the image of the beast should be killed.*

REVELATION 13:4–15

DEMONIC DECEPTION

Revelation vividly illustrates Satan's tendency for disguising himself as an angel of light. Notice how the antichrist gains the world's allegiance through an amazing spectacle. Imitating Christ's resurrection from the dead, the antichrist recovers after receiving a fatal wound (Revelation 13:3). But the false prophet's impersonation of Christ is even more ingenious. Like Christ, the false prophet performs astonishing miracles, including bringing a statue to life (Revelation 13:1–15). The demons also, with their dazzling miracles, deceive people and entrap the entire world (Revelation 16:1–14).

To prevent demonic miracles from leading people astray, the book of Revelation offers some insight on identifying demonic work. Babylon, described as the dwelling place of demons, is marked by three specific sins: idolatry, self-absorption, and self-sufficiency (Revelation 18:2–3, 7). Here, the distinction between what is godly and what is demonic becomes most obvious. Babylon represents the perversion of godly virtues: idolatry rather than worship of God, materialism rather than dependence on God, conceited thoughts of invincibility rather than the humility of the Lamb.

The book of Revelation clearly states that while demons may imitate God's power, they pervert his truth and character. This explains why the false prophet looks "like a lamb," but talks "like a dragon" (Revelation 13:11).

Need to Know
- A good example of demonic work can be seen in a prayer of Daniel. When the angel Michael arrived with the answer to Daniel's prayer, he claimed that a demon, "the prince of the kingdom of Persia," had hindered him on his journey (Daniel 10:10–13).
- According to Ephesians 6:12 there may be a hierarchy of demonic society: principalities, powers, rulers of the darkness of this world, spiritual wickedness in high places.

Think About It

- What elements of our society do you see as foundational weaknesses that will allow people to be deceived by false deities?
- From your experience, what are Satan's most effective disguises?

DAY 52

And there appeared a great wonder in heaven;
a woman clothed with the sun, and the moon under her feet,
and upon her head a crown of twelve stars: And she being with child
cried, travailing in birth, and pained to be delivered.
And there appeared another wonder in heaven;
and behold a great red dragon, having seven heads and ten horns,
and seven crowns upon his heads. And his tail drew the third part
of the stars of heaven, and did cast them to the earth:
and the dragon stood before the woman which was ready to be delivered,
for to devour her child as soon as it was born.
And she brought forth a man child, who was to rule all nations
with a rod of iron: and her child was caught up unto God,
and to his throne. And the woman fled into the wilderness,
where she hath a place prepared of God, that they should feed her
there a thousand two hundred and threescore days.
And there was war in heaven: Michael and his angels fought
against the dragon; and the dragon fought and his angels,
And prevailed not; neither was their place found any more in heaven.
And the great dragon was cast out, that old serpent, called the Devil,
and Satan, which deceiveth the whole world:
he was cast out into the earth, and his angels were cast out with him.

REVELATION 12:1–9

These shall make war with the Lamb,
and the Lamb shall overcome them: for he is Lord of lords,
and King of kings: and they that are with him are called,
and chosen, and faithful.

REVELATION 17:14

DEMONIC PERSECUTION

Vicious demonic attacks intensify after Michael, the archangel, ejects Satan from heaven (Revelation 12:7–17). The defeated Satan, knowing that his time is short, does everything in his power to destroy God's people (Revelation 12:12–17). It's important to remember, though, that the Lamb (Jesus) has already conquered these evil powers at the Cross, and he will one day demonstrate his power over them. Even as demonic forces viciously attack God's people, Revelation assures us that these evil powers have no future. They are already defeated! Their warfare against God is useless because Christ has already defeated them at the cross (Revelation 5:5; 12:1–11; 17:14; 19:1–21). At the final judgment, the demons will meet their ultimate destiny: the lake of fire and brimstone (Matthew 25:41; Revelation 20:10).

Need to Know
- The word for *fire* in the lake of fire is sometimes translated "burning sulphur." This place is called the second death because it is a final separation from God.
- The residents of the lake of fire will include the beast, the false prophet, Satan, death and hell and all those whose names are not found in the Book of Life.

Think About It
- How would you describe the kind of suffering that is caused by separation from God?
- What kind of alternate image would you paint of a place that was ultimate destruction?

Day 53

Wherefore take unto you the whole armour of God,
that ye may be able to withstand in the evil day, and having done all,
to stand. Stand therefore, having your loins girt about with truth,
and having on the breastplate of righteousness;
And your feet shod with the preparation of the gospel of peace;
Above all, taking the shield of faith, wherewith ye shall be able
to quench all the fiery darts of the wicked.
And take the helmet of salvation,
and the sword of the Spirit,
which is the word of God.
EPHESIANS 6:13–17

And I heard a loud voice saying in heaven,
Now is come salvation, and strength, and the kingdom of our God,
and the power of his Christ: for the accuser of our brethren is cast down,
which accused them before our God day and night.
And they overcame him by the blood of the Lamb,
and by the word of their testimony;
and they loved not their lives unto the death.
Therefore rejoice, ye heavens, and ye that dwell in them.
Woe to the inhabiters of the earth and of the sea! for the devil
is come down unto you, having great wrath,
because he knoweth that he hath but a short time.
REVELATION 12:10–12

Fighting Demons

Revelation's marvelous visions of the conquering Christ should remind us that God will ultimately bring evil to an end (Revelation 13:10). During the Tribulation, believers must remain focused on Jesus and only follow him. Demons can assume a beguiling appearance that easily leads people astray, so Christians must remain steeped in the word of God and obey Jesus (Ephesians 6:10–19; 1 Peter 5:8–9). God's people must not love their lives "unto the death" (Revelation 12:11). Believers know that demons are, in fact, doomed. Christ has defeated Satan. The demons are already conquered!

Need to Know
- For spiritual battle, Ephesians 6 tells us that God has given both defensive weapons (shield of faith, helmet of salvation) and offensive weapons (sword of the Spirit, the Word of God).
- Revelation 12:10–11 is a hymn of sorts. It is a celebration of God's victory over Satan. That victory was won when God expelled Satan from heaven. It was won with the death of Christ and validated through the martyrs of the faith. That victory will be finalized in the events described in Revelation.

Think About It
- If the demons are already doomed, then why do Christians sometimes feel so powerless against them?
- How will the world be different when evil is brought to an end?

Day 54

And there appeared a great wonder in heaven;
a woman clothed with the sun, and the moon under her feet,
and upon her head a crown of twelve stars:
And she being with child cried, travailing in birth,
and pained to be delivered.
And there appeared another wonder in heaven;
and behold a great red dragon, having seven heads and ten horns,
and seven crowns upon his heads.
And his tail drew the third part of the stars of heaven,
and did cast them to the earth:
and the dragon stood before the woman
which was ready to be delivered,
for to devour her child as soon as it was born.
REVELATION 12:1–4

And I saw one of his heads as it were wounded to death;
and his deadly wound was healed:
and all the world wondered after the beast.
REVELATION 13:3

Who Is the Antichrist?

Throughout history, many world leaders have been suggested as being the antichrist by concerned, but ultimately misguided, Christians. The glimpses we get of the antichrist in Scripture are veiled by mysterious imagery—a seven-headed monster with horns and blasphemous names inscribed in each one of its foreheads (Revelation 12:1–4). Though the Bible doesn't identify the antichrist by name, it does offer some intriguing descriptions of him. The apostle Paul calls him "the man of sin" (2 Thessalonians 2:3). Revelation describes him as "the beast" who emerges from the bottomless pit (Revelation 11:7). His entrance on the world stage will involve an astonishing spectacle: he will recover from a fatal wound (Revelation 13:3). We don't know how this event will be accomplished, but it's clear that his power will be derived from Satan himself. That power will extend beyond political and military affairs into the realm of religion. The antichrist will proclaim himself to be a god—and many will believe him.

Need to Know
- The crown of twelve stars worn by the woman in Revelation 12 is a victor's crown. The twelve stars represent the twelve tribes of Israel, though later the woman represents the whole of God's people, Jews and Gentiles alike.
- The child in Revelation 12 that the dragon waited to devour represented the Messiah, Jesus, the long awaited Savior of God's people.

Think About It
- Who are some modern leaders who cross back and forth between the lines of politics and religion?
- How do you think you will recognize the antichrist?

Day 55

Let no man deceive you by any means:
for that day shall not come,
except there come a falling away first,
and that man of sin be revealed, the son of perdition;
Who opposeth and exalteth himself above all that is called God,
or that is worshipped; so that he as God sitteth
in the temple of God, shewing himself that he is God.
Remember ye not, that, when I was yet with you,
I told you these things? And now ye know what withholdeth
that he might be revealed in his time.
For the mystery of iniquity doth already work:
only he who now letteth will let,
until he be taken out of the way.
2 THESSALONIANS 2:3–7

And I beheld another beast coming up out of the earth;
and he had two horns like a lamb, and he spake as a dragon.
And he exerciseth all the power of the first beast before him,
and causeth the earth and them which dwell therein
to worship the first beast, whose deadly wound was healed.
And he doeth great wonders, so that he maketh fire come down
from heaven on the earth in the sight of men,
And deceiveth them that dwell on the earth
by the means of those miracles which
he had power to do in the sight of the beast;
saying to them that dwell on the earth,
that they should make an image to the beast,
which had the wound by a sword, and did live.
And he had power to give life unto the image of the beast,
that the image of the beast should both speak,
and cause that as many as would not worship
the image of the beast should be killed.
REVELATION 13:11–15

HIS ORIGIN AND WORLD DOMINATION

The beast in Revelation doesn't enter the world's stage unexpectedly. He emerges from a great lineage of rebellion (2 Thessalonians 2:3, 7). Similarly, the beast rises from the bottomless pit, the abyss, which represents the satanic underworld (Revelation 11:7). The antichrist is the epitome of the satanic perversions and wickedness that are present in every age.

As a political figure, the antichrist becomes so powerful that opposing him is futile. All nations on earth serve him. Opposition against his rule is brutally suppressed. Only those who are branded with the beast's mark, showing their loyalty to him, will be able to participate in the world's economy (Mark 13:14, 20; Revelation 13:4, 7–8, 16–17).

Need to Know
- In Revelation, the beast is John's symbol for the antichrist while the Lamb is the symbol for Christ. The beast is a counterfeit building his own kingdom as he tries to take the place of Christ.
- The man of sin (or man of perdition) in 2 Thessalonians 2:3 is probably another reference to the antichrist.

Think About It
- How do you think you will be able to differentiate between the antichrist and a power hungry politician?
- What do you believe is the work of the satanic underworld today?

DAY 56

And there was given unto him
a mouth speaking great things and blasphemies;
and power was given unto him to continue forty and two months.
And he opened his mouth in blasphemy against God,
to blaspheme his name, and his tabernacle,
and them that dwell in heaven.
And it was given unto him to make war with the saints,
and to overcome them: and power was given him over all kindreds,
and tongues, and nations. And all that dwell upon the earth
shall worship him, whose names are not written
in the book of life of the Lamb
slain from the foundation of the world.
REVELATION 13:5–8

And deceiveth them that dwell on the earth
by the means of those miracles which he had power
to do in the sight of the beast;
saying to them that dwell on the earth,
that they should make an image to the beast,
which had the wound by a sword, and did live.
And he had power to give life unto the image of the beast,
that the image of the beast should both speak,
and cause that as many as would not worship
the image of the beast should be killed.
REVELATION 13:14–15

The Power of the Antichrist

The antichrist blasphemously exalts himself as God and ruthlessly persecutes those who don't worship his image (Daniel 7:21–27; 11:20–39; Mark 13:14, 20; 2 Thessalonians 2:3–4, 9–10). As a result, confessing Jesus as Lord may result in death (Revelation 13:5–8, 15). The antichrist is responsible for unleashing the Tribulation, the most intense period of persecution God's people will ever experience (Mark 13:14, 20).

Using spectacular miracles, the antichrist persuades the world to accept his false teachings (2 Thessalonians 2:9–11). Like Satan, who disguises himself as an angel of light, the beast seduces the world by supposedly imitating Christ's resurrection—when he recovers from a fatal wound (Revelation 13:3, 14).

Need to Know
- Miracles in the Bible were also referred to as *signs* and *wonders*. They signified an act of God, therefore his very presence and power. This is why miracles would give credence to the antichrist's claims to be from God. It would seem God's presence and power had enabled them.
- The antichrist will not be the first to punish those who don't worship the way he chooses. Christians in power through the ages have been guilty of the same persecution, just as they were persecuted by Rome in the first century and in many countries even today.

Think About It
- What consequences do you face now when you publicly confess Jesus as Lord?
- What kinds of consequences do you think would be the hardest for you to face, yet stay true to your convictions?

DAY 57

But the judgment shall sit,
and they shall take away his dominion,
to consume and to destroy it unto the end.
And the kingdom and dominion,
and the greatness of the kingdom under the whole heaven,
shall be given to the people of the saints of the most High,
whose kingdom is an everlasting kingdom,
and all dominions shall serve and obey him.
DANIEL 7:26–27

After this I beheld, and, lo, a great multitude,
which no man could number, of all nations, and kindreds,
and people, and tongues, stood before the throne,
and before the Lamb, clothed with white robes,
and palms in their hands;
And cried with a loud voice, saying,
Salvation to our God which sitteth upon the throne,
and unto the Lamb.
And all the angels stood round about the throne,
and about the elders and the four beasts,
and fell before the throne on their faces, and worshipped God,
Saying, Amen: Blessing, and glory, and wisdom,
and thanksgiving, and honour, and power, and might,
be unto our God for ever and ever. Amen.
REVELATION 7:9–12

THE GOAL OF THE ANTICHRIST

The antichrist's aim is principally religious. He exalts himself as nothing less than Jesus' rival. Note the parallels: both are worshiped (Revelation 13:8; 15:2–4); both are killed and come back to life (Revelation 13:3, 8); both have authority over all the nations (Revelation 7:9–10; 13:7); both mark their followers' heads (Revelation 13:16; 14:1). The antichrist not only ravages Christ's followers, he seeks to replace Christ.

Jesus will conquer the antichrist at the great battle of Armageddon. After that, the antichrist and his cohort, the false prophet, will be thrown into the fiery lake (Daniel 7:26–27; 11:36; Revelation 17:14; 19:19–21).

The antichrist reminds us that evil in our world is not simply the compilation of individual human wrongs. There is a "prince of evil" who arrogantly interferes with God's original intent for creation. Satan deceives us and seduces us into his wily schemes, like he has done since the Garden of Eden. Only one person can destroy Satan's power: the Lord Jesus Christ.

Need to Know
- The work of the antichrist will not be new work. Even when the serpent appeared to Eve in the Garden of Eden, he was counterfeiting God when he said, "God told you this, but that's not true. Trust what I tell you instead."
- One of the strongest descriptions of the antichrist outside of the book of Revelation is Paul's letter to the Thessalonians. These Christians had come to believe that they were already in the end times and Jesus' return was so imminent that some had already quit their jobs. Paul assured them that the antichrist would have to come before Christ's return (2 Thessalonians 2:2–12).

Think About It
- What was God's original intent for creation?
- Why do you think the antichrist's efforts are primarily religious rather than political?

Day 58

And he causeth all, both small and great, rich and poor, free and bond,
to receive a mark in their right hand, or in their foreheads:
And that no man might buy or sell, save he that had the mark,
or the name of the beast, or the number of his name.
Here is wisdom.
Let him that hath understanding count the number of the beast:
for it is the number of a man;
and his number is Six hundred threescore and six.
REVELATION 13:16–18

And the third angel followed them, saying with a loud voice,
If any man worship the beast and his image,
and receive his mark in his forehead, or in his hand,
The same shall drink of the wine of the wrath of God,
which is poured out without mixture into the cup of his indignation;
and he shall be tormented with fire and brimstone in the presence
of the holy angels, and in the presence of the Lamb:
And the smoke of their torment ascendeth up for ever and ever:
and they have no rest day nor night, who worship the beast
and his image, and whosoever receiveth the mark of his name.
Here is the patience of the saints: here are they that keep
the commandments of God, and the faith of Jesus.
REVELATION 14:9–12

THE MARK OF THE BEAST

In the end times, no one will be able to buy or sell anything without the brand of the beast (Revelation 13:16–17). Those who receive the brand of the beast will be readily identifiable. The mark will be stamped prominently on their right hands or foreheads. The mark will be the number 666 (Revelation 13:17–18). No one knows exactly what this number symbolizes.

Those who receive the mark of the beast will benefit economically for a brief time. Their short gain, however, will be quickly offset by the eternal consequences that await them. To receive the brand of the beast is, in essence, to worship the antichrist instead of the one true God. Revelation warns that those who accept the brand of the beast will have to endure God's cup of anger (Revelation 14:9–12; 20:7–15).

Need to Know
- For those who interpret Revelation as a description of events that happened in the first century, the mark of the beast could be a description of Nero, the Roman emperor of the first century who demanded worship, persecuted Christians, and blamed the burning of Rome on them.
- The Bible refers to God marking his own people. In Ezekiel's prophecy a mark is used by God to protect his people from a murderous judgment. These marks were on the foreheads of the people (Ezekiel 9:4–6). Earlier in Revelation, the 144,000 servants of God were sealed on their foreheads to provide some protection for them for the judgment (Revelation 7:1–4). When the plague of the locusts came, these marked people were protected from death, though not torment (Revelation 9:3–5).

Think About It
- What technologies that you see today could eventually be a part of the process of the taking the mark of the beast?
- What will differentiate the mark of the beast from some of our modern ways of buying and selling, like a check-cashing card?

Day 59

And I stood upon the sand of the sea,
and saw a beast rise up out of the sea,
having seven heads and ten horns,
and upon his horns ten crowns,
and upon his heads the name of blasphemy.
REVELATION 13:1

And I saw one of his heads as it were wounded to death;
and his deadly wound was healed:
and all the world wondered after the beast.
REVELATION 13:3

And he exerciseth all the power of the first beast before him,
and causeth the earth and them which dwell therein
to worship the first beast, whose deadly wound was healed.
REVELATION 13:12

And deceiveth them that dwell on the earth by the means
of those miracles which he had power to do in the sight of the beast;
saying to them that dwell on the earth,
that they should make an image to the beast,
which had the wound by a sword, and did live.
REVELATION 13:14

THE BEAST: MAYBE NERO?

Many postmillennialists believe that the prophecies regarding the antichrist have already been fulfilled. Some link the beast in Revelation with the Roman emperoro Nero, who committed suicide and who was widely expected to come back to life and reclaim his throne. Those who interpret the antichrist as Nero believe the seven-headed beast symbolizes the evil Roman Empire, because the city of Rome was built on seven hills (Revelation 17:9). Thus, the antichrist was a Roman emperor.

Certainly, there are parallels between the beast and Roman emperors. But this identification of the antichrist with Nero has been seriously challenged. Revelation indicates that the beast itself—the evil empire itself—receives the fatal wound (Revelation 13:3, 12, 14). Nero's suicide hardly endangered the Roman Empire. Today, many doubt whether the antichrist was Nero or any other Roman emperor.

Need to Know

- Nero was the fifth Roman emperor, the last in the family line of Julius Caesar. He ruled from A.D. 54 until his death in A.D. 68. While his reign began peacefully, it disintegrated into destruction and death. Nero himself was a suspect in the burning of a large part of Rome in A.D. 64. He blamed the Christians, thus initiating horrible persecution.
- The name *Caesar* was originally a family name, that of Julius Caesar, who never actually held the title emperor. The name became a title used by emperors such as Augustus and Tiberius, who reigned in the time of Christ.

Think About It

- What principles do you follow in deciding whether Scriptures are prophetic of the future or merely descriptions of the past?
- What political leaders in your lifetime most remind you of Nero, famous for destruction more than restoration? How should Christians stand against such leaders?

DAY 60

And I stood upon the sand of the sea,
and saw a beast rise up out of the sea,
having seven heads and ten horns,
and upon his horns ten crowns,
and upon his heads the name of blasphemy.
And the beast which I saw was like unto a leopard,
and his feet were as the feet of a bear,
and his mouth as the mouth of a lion:
and the dragon gave him his power,
and his seat, and great authority.

REVELATION 13:1–2

And here is the mind which hath wisdom.
The seven heads are seven mountains, on which the woman sitteth.
And there are seven kings: five are fallen, and one is,
and the other is not yet come; and when he cometh,
he must continue a short space. And the beast that was, and is not,
even he is the eighth, and is of the seven, and goeth into perdition.
And the ten horns which thou sawest are ten kings, which have received
no kingdom as yet; but receive power as kings one hour with the beast.
These have one mind, and shall give their power and strength unto the
beast. These shall make war with the Lamb,
and the Lamb shall overcome them: for he is Lord of lords,
and King of kings: and they that are with him are called,
and chosen, and faithful.

REVELATION 17:9–14

THE BEAST: A WESTERN LEADER?

Dispensationalists have outlined a detailed scenario for the antichrist. He emerges as the leader of the restored Roman Empire and guarantees the security of Israel (Daniel 7:8, 21–27; 9:24–27; Revelation 17:9–14). After being assassinated, he is restored to life. This only enhances his claims to deity and his goal of world domination. When he exalts himself in the temple at Jerusalem, he reveals his blasphemous and malicious character. His persecution causes Israel to turn to the Messiah. The Tribulation climaxes with military forces converging on Israel to defeat the antichrist.

Some readers question this type of interpretation because it has little biblical evidence to support it. For example, the identification of the beast as the Roman Empire ignores the fact that the beast combines the attributes of all four creatures described in Daniel 7 (Revelation 13:1–2).

Need to Know

- The four creatures, or beasts, in Daniel 7 were a lion with eagle wings, a bear with ribs in its mouth, a leopard with four wings, and a ten-horned beast with a human face. Each of these beasts represented a world power.
- While there is much disagreement here about what images represent which reality, the truth remains that evil will rise against God and will seem to be winning—but in the end God will triumph.

Think About It

- When you are faced with differing opinions on Scripture interpretation, as above, what do you use to make your decisions?
- When you apply the truth of Scripture to your life, how do you deal with the unexplainable details you find there?

DAY 61

And Jesus answered and said unto them,
Take heed that no man deceive you.
For many shall come in my name, saying,
I am Christ; and shall deceive many.
MATTHEW 24:4–5

Humble yourselves therefore under the mighty hand of God,
that he may exalt you in due time:
Casting all your care upon him; for he careth for you.
Be sober, be vigilant; because your adversary the devil,
as a roaring lion, walketh about, seeking whom he may devour:
Whom resist stedfast in the faith, knowing that the same afflictions
are accomplished in your brethren that are in the world.
But the God of all grace, who hath called us unto his eternal glory
by Christ Jesus, after that ye have suffered a while,
make you perfect, stablish, strengthen, settle you.
To him be glory and dominion for ever and ever. Amen.
1 PETER 5:6–11

BE WATCHFUL

We should never let various theories on how prophecies are interpreted to frustrate us. The advocates of all of these theories are following Jesus' command to be watchful (Matthew 24:4–5). They're all looking forward to Jesus' return. Each idea about the identity of the antichrist warns the church to be wary of false prophets—those who seek to lead the church away from Jesus.

Are you being watchful? Remember Peter's warning: "Be sober, be vigilant; because your adversary the devil, as a roaring lion, walketh about, seeking whom he may devour" (1 Peter 5:8).

Need to Know
- Both Paul and Peter reminded their readers that Jesus would come as a thief in the night. In this way, they encouraged the first-century Christians not to assume they knew when Christ would come, but to live in readiness (1 Thessalonians 5:2; 2 Peter 3:10).
- New Testament writers often used the word *asleep* to describe moral indifference. This adds color to the picture of Christ coming as a thief in the night. Those who are *asleep* will not be ready (Mark 13:34–37; Romans 13:10–14).

Think About It
- What do you do to protect yourself from false teaching or falling away from the faith?
- How would you describe your level of readiness for the return of Christ?

Day 62

And I beheld another beast coming up out of the earth;
and he had two horns like a lamb, and he spake as a dragon.
And he exerciseth all the power of the first beast before him,
and causeth the earth and them which dwell therein to worship
the first beast, whose deadly wound was healed.
And he doeth great wonders, so that he maketh fire come down
from heaven on the earth in the sight of men,
And deceiveth them that dwell on the earth by the means
of those miracles which he had power to do in the sight of the beast;
saying to them that dwell on the earth, that they should make
an image to the beast, which had the wound by a sword, and did live.
And he had power to give life unto the image of the beast,
that the image of the beast should both speak, and cause that
as many as would not worship the image of the beast should be killed.
And he causeth all, both small and great, rich and poor, free and bond,
to receive a mark in their right hand, or in their foreheads:
And that no man might buy or sell, save he that had the mark,
or the name of the beast, or the number of his name.
Here is wisdom. Let him that hath understanding count
the number of the beast: for it is the number of a man;
and his number is Six hundred threescore and six.

Revelation 13:11–18

666

"Let him that hath understanding count the number of the beast: for it is the number of a man" (Revelation 13:18). Throughout its history, the church has assigned numerical values to the letters of names in order to identify the beast. Some proposed figures include *Lateinos,* which alludes to the entire Roman Empire; *Neron Kaisar,* under whose direction the church suffered intense persecution; and *Teitan,* for Titus, the Roman Emperor who destroyed Jerusalem in A.D. 70. The number continues to be linked with various world leaders, institutions, and types of economic transactions.

Many conservative commentators support another proposal. As a representative of apocalyptic literature, the book of Revelation overflows with symbolism. John uses the number *seven* in the book as a symbol of God's perfection. Conversely, the number *six* symbolizes human imperfection. Six is one less than the number seven; three sixes, 666, implies a trinity of imperfection—a perverse parody of the perfection of number seven.

Need to Know

- Numerology is a study of numbers assigning numerical values to the letter of names. Numerology finds meaning in terms of abilities and character tendencies based on numbers such as date of birth. It is associated with the study of astrology.
- This number of the beast, 666, is possibly one of the most famous numbers from the Bible, though there are many others.

Think About It

- What does the number 666 mean to you?
- Do the symbols of Revelation enlighten you, intrigue you, confuse you? How so?

Day 63

For the Son of man shall come in the glory
of his Father with his angels;
and then he shall reward every man according to his works.
MATTHEW 16:27

Who will render to every man according to his deeds:
To them who by patient continuance in well doing
seek for glory and honour and immortality, eternal life:
But unto them that are contentious, and do not obey the truth,
but obey unrighteousness, indignation and wrath,
Tribulation and anguish, upon every soul of man that doeth evil,
of the Jew first, and also of the Gentile; But glory, honour, and peace,
to every man that worketh good, to the Jew first, and also to the Gentile:
For there is no respect of persons with God.
ROMANS 2:6–11

GREAT INJUSTICE

News reports of genocide, sexual abuse, and other unimaginable horrors bombard us every day. The images and stories can harden our hearts. We can even become used to violence and injustice. But God didn't create us that way. Injustice and suffering should always leave us asking: "Who will right these wrongs? When will the wicked be judged? Will justice ever be established?"

God created us accountable to him, the moral Judge of the cosmos. Humanity's rebellion against God is the gravest evil of all and the root of all injustice. God has promised that he will punish all sin (Romans 2:6–11; 12:19). Hell is the horrific and tragic place where the wicked will be paid back for how they have rejected God and mistreated their fellow human beings (Matthew 13:41–42; 16:27).

Sin must be punished. That fact creates a serious human predicament—all have sinned, and so all are under God's judgment (Romans 3:23). The Good News is that God, in the person of Jesus Christ, came to this rebellious world and suffered the punishment for those who have "faith in Christ's blood" (Romans 3:25; 2 Corinthians 5:21). Without God's awesome love, people would have no hope.

Need to Know
- God has never let his people off the hook in terms of confronting society. The Old Testament prophets spoke often against poor treatment of the poor and unfortunate.
- New Testament writers often defined Christian faith by how that faith is acted out in the world. While we will never create "heaven on earth," we are not relieved of the responsibility to fight wickedness in our world.

Think About It
- What societal wrongs can you address and do something to change?
- When you observe your community, what evidence do you see that humanity's rebellion against God is the root of all injustice?

Day 64

But the children of the kingdom shall be cast out into outer darkness:
there shall be weeping and gnashing of teeth.
MATTHEW 8:12

And if thine eye offend thee, pluck it out,
and cast it from thee: it is better for thee to enter into life with one eye,
rather than having two eyes to be cast into hell fire.
MATTHEW 18:9

And the devil that deceived them was cast into the lake of fire
and brimstone, where the beast and the false prophet are,
and shall be tormented day and night for ever and ever.
REVELATION 20:10

And death and hell were cast into the lake of fire.
This is the second death. And whosoever was not found
written in the book of life was cast into the lake of fire.
REVELATION 20:14–15

THE LAKE OF FIRE

At the final judgment, Satan and all of the wicked are cast into the lake of burning sulfur to be "tormented day and night forever and ever" (Revelation 19:20; 20:10, 14–15). Throughout Scripture, fire and burning sulfur are used to portray God's searing holiness as he exacts retribution for evil (Genesis 19:24; Ezekiel 38:22; Hebrews 10:27–31; Revelation 14:9–11). Much speculation has focused on whether these are literal fires. Many biblical scholars, including the Protestant Reformers, noted that a literal fire conflicts with the image of hell as "outer darkness" (Matthew 8:12). Whatever the view, hell is a horrific reality. Jesus' repeated warnings cannot be ignored: "And if thine eye offend thee, pluck it out, and cast it from thee: it is better for thee to enter into life with one eye, rather than. . .be cast into hell fire" (Matthew 18:9).

Need to Know
- Jesus' recommendation to get rid of whatever causes you to lose faith came on the heels of admonition to leaders. He was speaking with his disciples and had just reminded them to come to God as a child. Those who lead have an even greater responsibility to rid their lives of sin.
- The imagery of the lake of fire was probably drawn from the fires in the Valley of Hinnom. It was this valley outside of Jerusalem that Jesus called Gehenna, the outer darkness.

Think About It
- What would you consider the worst thing about hell?
- What are your greatest temptations to sin?

TABLE: FAST FACTS ON HELL

Though the Bible spares us graphic depictions of hell, it does tell us enough about this fiery lake of sulfur to give even the most jaded readers cause to consider their destinies. Here are some brief descriptions of this horrific place.

Characteristics of Hell	Reference
Crying and extreme pain ("wailing and gnashing of teeth")	Matthew 13:42; 24:51
Endless torture	Revelation 14:11
Eternal shame and disgrace	Daniel 12:2
Fire	Revelation 20:15
God's anger and fury	Revelation 14:10
Punishment	Matthew 25:46
Remembering and remorse	Luke 16:19–31
Second death	Revelation 2:11; 20:6
Thirst	Luke 16:24
Unquenchable fire	Matthew 3:12; 13:41–42; Mark 9:43
Prison	Matthew 5:22–26; 18:34–35; Jude 6; Revelation 20:7, 10, 14–15; 21:8
Isolation from God	Matthew 8:12; 22:13
Utter exclusion from God and the righteous	Matthew 25:12, 41; John 5:29; 2 Thessalonians 1:9
Utter ruin	Psalm 88:12; Isaiah 14:11; Matthew 8:12; 25:30; Mark 9:48; Luke 9:25; Jude 13
Eternity	Mark 9:48; Revelation 14:11; 20:10

Day 65

When the Son of man shall come in his glory,
and all the holy angels with him, then shall he sit upon the throne
of his glory: And before him shall be gathered all nations:
and he shall separate them one from another,
as a shepherd divideth his sheep from the goats:
And he shall set the sheep on his right hand,
but the goats on the left.
MATTHEW 25:31–33

Then shall he say also unto them on the left hand,
Depart from me, ye cursed, into everlasting fire,
prepared for the devil and his angels:
For I was an hungred, and ye gave me no meat:
I was thirsty, and ye gave me no drink:
I was a stranger, and ye took me not in: naked,
and ye clothed me not: sick, and in prison, and ye visited me not.
Then shall they also answer him, saying, Lord, when saw we thee
an hungred, or athirst, or a stranger, or naked, or sick,
or in prison, and did not minister unto thee?
Then shall he answer them, saying, V
erily I say unto you, Inasmuch as ye did it not
to one of the least of these, ye did it not to me.
And these shall go away into everlasting punishment:
but the righteous into life eternal.
MATTHEW 25:41–46

FIRE AND DARKNESS

Although Scripture uses images of fiery brimstone and sulfur, destruction, and darkness for hell (Matthew 7:13; 18:8; Jude 13; Revelation 14:10), Scripture doesn't describe in excruciating detail the awful fate of hell. Actually, Jesus says more about hell than any other biblical figure. He used the Greek word *gehenna* to describe hell. The word alludes to the valley of Ben Hinnom, where Old Testament Israelites sacrificed their children to false gods and later burned their garbage and refuse (Jeremiah 7:31).

Jesus repeatedly warns that hell is a fate far worse than physical death. Scripture consistently describes hell as a place where one is utterly alone, rejected by one's Creator, and excluded from his loving presence (Matthew 25:12, 41; Luke 13:24–28; 2 Thessalonians 1:8–9).

Need to Know
- "As a shepherd divideth his sheep" (Matthew 25:32), uses the Greek verb *aphorizo* for "divide," meaning to mark off by boundaries or limits, and denotes separation and severing.
- In ancient Canaan, pagan worship of the god Molech was prevalent, along with child sacrifices. It was against God's law for the Israelites to sacrifice children. When the Israelites were tempted to worship Molech, it was with the grave threat of judgment from God.

Think About It
- What do you think people fear most about hell—the physical suffering or the separation from God?
- When you think about separation from God (the essence of hell), what comes to mind?

DAY 66

Take ye heed, watch and pray: for ye know not when the time is.
For the Son of man is as a man taking a far journey,
who left his house, and gave authority to his servants,
and to every man his work, and commanded the porter to watch.
Watch ye therefore: for ye know not when the master of the house cometh,
at even, or at midnight, or at the cockcrowing, or in the morning:
Lest coming suddenly he find you sleeping.
And what I say unto you I say unto all, Watch.
MARK 13:33–37

Jesus saith unto him, I am the way, the truth, and the life:
no man cometh unto the Father, but by me.
JOHN 14:6

For it pleased the Father that in him should all fulness dwell;
And, having made peace through the blood of his cross,
by him to reconcile all things unto himself; by him,
I say, whether they be things in earth, or things in heaven.
And you, that were sometime alienated and enemies in your mind
by wicked works, yet now hath he reconciled in the body
of his flesh through death, to present you holy
and unblameable and unreproveable in his sight.
COLOSSIANS 1:19–22

OTHER VIEWS ON HELL

Some people believe the concept of hell contradicts the idea of Jesus' love for people. *Universalists* believe that everyone, even the wicked, will finally be embraced by God's love.

But universalism hardly agrees with Jesus' own pronouncements. When Jesus offers salvation, he is providing God's unique supernatural intervention (John 14:6). Christians profess that salvation is by grace alone. It reflects God's free decision to save us. Furthermore, Jesus urges us to be ready for his return—to accept his free offer of salvation before it's too late (Matthew 25:13; Mark 13:33–37)—for God's gracious offer of saving love is not an eternal offer (Matthew 25:41). Christ will return in judgment (2 Thessalonians 1:7–10). At that time, it will be too late. Scripture rejects the idea of a second chance after death. Decisions regarding salvation are confined to this life (Hebrews 9:27).

Annihilationists insist that the biblical imagery of a consuming fire implies that the wicked are consumed. Therefore, hell's duration is limited, not everlasting.

Need to Know
- There is a parallel in the Bible between physical death and spiritual death. Adam brought sin into the world. Jesus brought redemption. Adam's legacy is that we all die a physical death. Jesus' legacy is that we are saved from a spiritual death if we choose to be (Romans 5:12; 1 Corinthians 15:22).
- In the Bible salvation comes to us by God's grace, through faith, which is also a gift of God. Yet authentic faith will prompt us to good deeds. There is a balance in which one must be present to validate the other, but we cannot earn our salvation through good deeds (Ephesians 2:8–9; James 2:17).

Think About It
- Why do you think Jesus taught so much about hell?

TABLE: THE INHABITANTS OF HELL

Who will be in hell? Red creatures with pitchforks and horns? Although popular perceptions of hell may make it seem like a fictional place, the Bible emphasizes that hell is very real—a place where no one wants to be. Hell won't be inhabited by mythical beasts and monsters—tragically, it will be filled with people who have willfully rebelled against God. The only way to escape this awful place is to accept God's free gift of salvation and believe in his Son (Romans 3:23).

Who Is in Hell?	Reference
All who hold on to their sins of cowardliness, unfaithfulness, murder, sexual immorality, sorcery, idolatry, and lying	Revelation 21:8, 27
All who accept the rewards of sin rather than the gift of everlasting life from God through Jesus Christ	Romans 6:23
The devil and his angels, for whom it was originally prepared	Matthew 25:41; 2 Peter 2:4
All who have failed to recognize their sin in not treating others as Jesus requested	Matthew 25:31–46
The beast and the false prophet, servants of the devil in the end times	Revelation 20:10
Idolaters, covetous, sexually immoral people	1 Corinthians 6:9–11
All whose names are not written in the Book of Life	Revelation 20:15

Day 67

Now then we are ambassadors for Christ,
as though God did beseech you by us: we pray you in Christ's stead,
be ye reconciled to God. For he hath made him to be sin for us,
who knew no sin; that we might be made
the righteousness of God in him.
2 CORINTHIANS 5:20–21

For even hereunto were ye called: because Christ
also suffered for us, leaving us an example,
that ye should follow his steps:
Who did no sin, neither was guile found in his mouth:
Who, when he was reviled, reviled not again;
when he suffered, he threatened not;
but committed himself to him that judgeth righteously:
Who his own self bare our sins in his own body on the tree,
that we, being dead to sins, should live unto righteousness:
by whose stripes ye were healed. For ye were as sheep going astray;
but are now returned unto the Shepherd and Bishop of your souls.
1 PETER 2:21–25

JESUS SPEAKS ON ETERNITY

In Matthew 25:46, Jesus discusses the two futures of everlasting life and eternal punishment. He uses the same adjective, *eternal,* for each one. Both heaven and hell are eternal—forever. Elsewhere, Jesus states clearly that hell is a place where "the fire is not quenched" (Mark 9:48). And Revelation says the wicked are punished "for ever and ever" (Revelation 14:11; 20:10). Every sin is an offense against the infinite God, and the penalty for that sin is also infinite. That is why the only one who can pay for our infinite debt is God's Son, Jesus (2 Corinthians 5:21; 1 Peter 2:24).

As the Son of God who knows all things, Jesus clearly warns us that hell is a horrible reality (Matthew 8:10–12; 25:31–46; Luke 13:24–28). Hell was one reason why Jesus was willing to humble himself and suffer for us on the cross. Jesus wants to save us from ourselves—from our own rebellion against God and its tragic consequences.

Need to Know
- The Greek word *aionos* is the word used for "everlasting" and "eternal" in Matthew 25:46, denoting a duration of undefined time, but refers to persons or things which are endless in their nature.
- The significance of Jesus' sacrifice turns on his sinlessness. He was the pure Lamb of God, the one who lived according to the true law of God. The sinless one paid the price for our sins.

Think About It
- How do you feel about Jesus' teachings about hell?
- Why is sin so abhorrent to God?

Day 68

Ye shall know them by their fruits.
Do men gather grapes of thorns, or figs of thistles?
Even so every good tree bringeth forth good fruit;
but a corrupt tree bringeth forth evil fruit.
A good tree cannot bring forth evil fruit,
neither can a corrupt tree bring forth good fruit.
Every tree that bringeth not forth good fruit is hewn down,
and cast into the fire.
Wherefore by their fruits ye shall know them.
MATTHEW 7:16–20

A good man out of the good treasure of the heart
bringeth forth good things:
and an evil man out of the evil treasure
bringeth forth evil things.
But I say unto you,
That every idle word that men shall speak,
they shall give account thereof in the day of judgment.
For by thy words thou shalt be justified,
and by thy words thou shalt be condemned.
MATTHEW 12:35–37

Verily, verily, I say unto you,
He that heareth my word, and believeth on him that sent me,
hath everlasting life, and shall not come into condemnation;
but is passed from death unto life. Verily, verily, I say unto you,
The hour is coming, and now is, when the dead shall hear
the voice of the Son of God: and they that hear shall live.
For as the Father hath life in himself;
so hath he given to the Son to have life in himself;
and hath given him authority to execute judgment also,
because he is the Son of man. Marvel not at this: for the hour is coming,
in the which all that are in the graves shall hear his voice,
and shall come forth; they that have done good,
unto the resurrection of life; and they that have done evil,
unto the resurrection of damnation.
JOHN 5:24–29

Standing Before God

Everyone—the living and the dead, people as well as angels—will stand before Christ (Hebrews 12:23; 1 Peter 4:5; Jude 6) to be judged according to the things they have done (Matthew 16:27; Romans 2:6; Revelation 22:12). Nothing can be hidden from God, not even our "secret thoughts" (Romans 2:16). Every deed will be examined, from idle words to not helping the hungry (Matthew 12:36; 25:31–46).

Because everyone has sinned (Romans 3:23), God's judgment will fall on all people—from murderers (Revelation 21:8) to pious hypocrites (Matthew 23:29–33), to those who fail to help the poor (Matthew 25:31–46). Only those people who are saved by Jesus' redemptive work will escape God's punishment. Christ, the Judge, has already suffered God's punishment for sin. Those who have faith in him are forgiven of their sins (John 3:18; 5:24; Romans 3:25; 2 Corinthians 5:21). And what God has already forgiven, he will not recall (Isaiah 43:25; Jeremiah 31:34). That's why believers in Christ may stand before the Lord without fear (Romans 8:33–34; Ephesians 5:27).

While our works cannot save us, they aren't unimportant to God (Philippians 3:9). Though no other foundation "can no man lay than that is laid, which is Jesus Christ" (1 Corinthians 3:11), our faith must be active in forgiveness, love, and good works (Matthew 7:17–19). These works are the basis for the believer's rewards (1 Corinthians 3:10–15).

Need to Know
- The word that Paul used in Romans 3:23 for *sin* means "to miss the mark, to fail in the duty."
- God has set a standard for us to live up to. Jesus came to give us an example. We may rightly concentrate on singular behaviors that we call sin, but our sin is the failure to live up to God's expectations of us. Jesus spanned the gap between our failures and those expectations.

Think About It
- When you think of standing before God, what comes first to mind?

DAY 69

But God, who is rich in mercy,
for his great love wherewith he loved us,
Even when we were dead in sins,
hath quickened us together with Christ, (by grace ye are saved);
and hath raised us up together,
and made us sit together in heavenly places in Christ Jesus:
That in the ages to come he might shew
the exceeding riches of his grace in his kindness
toward us through Christ Jesus.
For by grace are ye saved through faith;
and that not of yourselves: it is the gift of God: not of works,
lest any man should boast. For we are his workmanship,
created in Christ Jesus unto good works,
which God hath before ordained that we should walk in them.
EPHESIANS 2:4–10

And I saw a great white throne, and him that sat on it,
from whose face the earth and the heaven fled away;
and there was found no place for them. And I saw the dead,
small and great, stand before God; and the books were opened:
and another book was opened, which is the book of life:
and the dead were judged out of those things
which were written in the books, according to their works.
And the sea gave up the dead which were in it;
and death and hell delivered up the dead which were in them:
and they were judged every man according to their works.
And death and hell were cast into the lake of fire.
This is the second death.
And whosoever was not found written
in the book of life was cast into the lake of fire.
REVELATION 20:11–15

WILL SOME SUFFER MORE THAN OTHERS?

Describing the Lord's final judgment on the lost, Revelation 20:12 says, "The dead were judged out of those things which were written in the books, according to their works." The suggestion here is that Christ will consider people's earthly works before he passes final judgment on them. We know that works can do nothing to save a person (Ephesians 2:8–9). We also know that only lost people will be gathered at the great white throne judgment in Revelation 20. Therefore, it seems reasonable to conclude that Christ will impose different degrees of punishment based on people's works. Christ is a completely righteous and just Judge; he will assign each person the exact punishment he or she deserves.

Need to Know
- Humanity is created in God's image, and therefore all are morally accountable to God in a way that no other part of creation is.
- It is not humanity's guilt that will be decided at the last judgment. We are all guilty. What will be decided is whether we have accepted the redemption in Christ which God offers.

Think About It
- What kind of behaviors do you think will receive the harshest punishment?
- Do you feel free from fear of judgment?

Day 70

For, behold, I create new heavens and a new earth:
and the former shall not be remembered, nor come into mind.
But be ye glad and rejoice for ever in that which I create: for, behold,
I create Jerusalem a rejoicing, and her people a joy.
And I will rejoice in Jerusalem, and joy in my people:
and the voice of weeping shall be no more heard in her,
nor the voice of crying.
Isaiah 65:17–19

Let not your heart be troubled:
ye believe in God, believe also in me.
In my Father's house are many mansions: if it were not so,
I would have told you. I go to prepare a place for you.
And if I go and prepare a place for you, I will come again,
and receive you unto myself; that where I am, there ye may be also.
And whither I go ye know, and the way ye know.
John 14:1–4

And I saw a new heaven and a new earth:
for the first heaven and the first earth were passed away;
and there was no more sea. And I John saw the holy city,
new Jerusalem, coming down from God out of heaven,
prepared as a bride adorned for her husband.
And I heard a great voice out of heaven saying,
Behold, the tabernacle of God is with men,
and he will dwell with them, and they shall be his people,
and God himself shall be with them, and be their God.
And God shall wipe away all tears from their eyes;
and there shall be no more death, neither sorrow,
nor crying, neither shall there be any more pain:
for the former things are passed away.
REVELATION 21:1–4

It's Perfect

When Scripture uses the word *heaven,* it may mean the whole cosmos, the sky (the realm of the planets and stars), or God's dwelling place. But when Scripture describes the place where believers will live for eternity as *heaven,* it's referring to God's dwelling place. Jesus went to God's dwelling place, to stand in a position of authority beside God the Father (Acts 7:55–56). There, he is preparing a glorious place for all those who believe in him (John 14:2–3).

Following the final judgment and the defeat of all evil, God will create "a new heaven and a new earth" because the old earth and the old universe will have disappeared (Isaiah 65:17; 2 Peter 3:10; Revelation 21:1). Then, the place that Jesus has prepared for us—the New Jerusalem—will descend from the sky onto the new earth. In this sparkling, new city, God will finally live among his holy people. The New Jerusalem will be God's new dwelling place, and we will live with God in that city forever (Revelation 22:5).

Need to Know
- It was King David that made Jerusalem the spiritual center as well as the political capital city of Judah. The city had already existed as the city of Jebus.
- Some Christians see this new Jerusalem as a literal city. Others, just as convinced of God's judgment and restoration, see the new Jerusalem as the church of Christ, finally perfected when Christ returns.

Think About It
- In what way does the modern church feel weary and tired, ready for a spiritual overhaul into a new creation?
- What hope does it give you to think of a new world restored by God?

TABLE: FAST FACTS ON HEAVEN

Have you ever dreamed about what living with God in eternity would be like? Fluffy clouds? Golden halos? Streets of gold? What will it be like to enjoy God's presence? In other words, what will heaven be like? The apostle John caught a glimpse of heaven in a breathtaking vision of the new Jerusalem. Here is what he saw:

The holy city is called the new Jerusalem	Revelation 21:2
Its overall appearance is made of gray quartz (jasper) and pure gold	Revelation 21:11, 18
The city is shaped like a huge equilateral cube	Revelation 21:16
The size of the structure is about 1,400 miles on each side	Revelation 21:16
The foundation of the city is composed of twelve layers of stones inlaid with jewels	Revelation 21:19–20
The names of each of the twelve apostles are engraved on the foundation layers	Revelation 21:19–20
The walls around the city are built of gray quartz	Revelation 21:18
The walls are over 200 feet high	Revelation 21:17
There are twelve solid pearl gates (three on each wall)	Revelation 21:12, 21
Each gate is named for one the Israel's twelve tribes	Revelation 21:12
The river of life flows in the city	Revelation 22:1
The tree of life grows in the city	Revelation 2:7; 22:19
The throne room of God occupies the central palace	Revelation 4:2; 22:1
The city's main street is made of transparent gold	Revelation 21:21
The dazzling light of the city comes from God's glory	Revelation 21:11, 23; 22:5
God himself will live in the city among his people	Revelation 21:3; 22:4
God's people will live in the new Jerusalem in the presence of God forever	Revelation 22:5

Day 71

Having the glory of God: and her light was like unto a stone
most precious, even like a jasper stone, clear as crystal;
And had a wall great and high, and had twelve gates,
and at the gates twelve angels, and names written thereon,
which are the names of the twelve tribes of the children of Israel:
On the east three gates; on the north three gates;
on the south three gates; and on the west three gates.
And the wall of the city had twelve foundations,
and in them the names of the twelve apostles of the Lamb.
And he that talked with me had a golden reed to measure the city,
and the gates thereof, and the wall thereof.
And the city lieth foursquare,
and the length is as large as the breadth:
and he measured the city with the reed, twelve thousand furlongs.
The length and the breadth and the height of it are equal.
And he measured the wall thereof,
an hundred and forty and four cubits,
according to the measure of a man, that is, of the angel.
And the building of the wall of it was of jasper:
and the city was pure gold, like unto clear glass.
And the foundations of the wall of the city were garnished
with all manner of precious stones.
The first foundation was jasper; the second, sapphire;
the third, a chalcedony; the fourth, an emerald;
the fifth, sardonyx; the sixth, sardius; the seventh, chrysolite;
the eighth, beryl; the ninth, a topaz; the tenth, a chrysoprasus;
the eleventh, a jacinth; the twelfth, an amethyst.
And the twelve gates were twelve pearls;
every several gate was of one pearl: and the street of the city
was pure gold, as it were transparent glass.

REVELATION 21:11–21

THE NEW JERUSALEM

Do you ever yearn for true peace in your family, in your community, or in your nation? Do you dream of the day when you can finally put away your frantic work and truly rest? These hopes and longings will only be satisfied in heaven. Only in heaven will we be able to truly rest—to simply enjoy our Creator's presence. As John's images of golden streets, foundations of precious jewels and gates of pearl suggest, the New Jerusalem will be far beyond anything we have experienced or imagined. It will be a place of eternal joy and happiness—a place the Scripture calls the heavenly Jerusalem (Hebrews 12:22; 13:14).

In this heavenly Jerusalem, "there shall be no more curse" (Revelation 22:3). Just as God was present with Adam and Eve before the fall, so in the New Jerusalem God will dwell among his people (Revelation 21:3). All evil is eliminated in the New Jerusalem, and the possibility of sin is erased (Jude 1:24; Revelation 21:27). There is no "sorrow or crying" (Revelation 21:4). We will never be hungry or thirsty again (Revelation 7:16). Without the sinful hurdles of our present age, we will finally experience life as it's meant to be experienced, forever and ever (Revelation 22:1–2).

Need to Know

- The Old Testament prophet Isaiah gave a description similar to John's when he prophesied Jerusalem's restoration. He spoke of an eventual city made of precious jewels and filled with peace (Isaiah 54:1–14).
- In this new Jerusalem God will be the source of light, and Jesus, the Lamb, will be the lamp that sheds that light (Revelation 21:23).

Think About It

- How do you think your relationship and interactions with God will be different in the new Jerusalem?
- What experiences of your life have given you a little glimpse of what heaven will be?

Day 72

After this I looked, and, behold, a door was opened in heaven:
and the first voice which I heard was as it were
of a trumpet talking with me; which said,
Come up hither, and I will shew thee things
which must be hereafter.
And immediately I was in the spirit:
and, behold, a throne was set in heaven,
and one sat on the throne.
And he that sat was to look upon
like a jasper and a sardine stone:
and there was a rainbow round about the throne,
in sight like unto an emerald.
And round about the throne were four and twenty seats:
and upon the seats I saw four and twenty elders sitting,
clothed in white raiment;
and they had on their heads crowns of gold.
And out of the throne proceeded lightnings and thunderings
and voices: and there were seven lamps of fire burning
before the throne, which are the seven Spirits of God.
And before the throne there was a sea of glass like unto crystal:
and in the midst of the throne, and round about the throne,
were four beasts full of eyes before and behind.
And the first beast was like a lion, and the second beast like a calf,
and the third beast had a face as a man,
and the fourth beast was like a flying eagle.
And the four beasts had each of them six wings about him;
and they were full of eyes within: and they rest not day and night,
saying, Holy, holy, holy, Lord God Almighty,
which was, and is, and is to come.

REVELATION 4:1–8

WHAT WILL HEAVEN BE LIKE?

John provides a fantastic and rather baffling description of heaven and the throne of God in Revelation 4. It's certainly possible that John's depiction can be taken literally. Heaven may very well be a place of emerald rainbows, gold crowns, and a crystal sea. After all, God is capable of creating anything he desires. More likely, though, John was simply using the limited descriptive words and images available to him to communicate heaven's indescribable appearance.

All beauty comes from God. Anything that corrupts or taints beauty is the result of sin. So absolute beauty—breathtaking spectacle beyond our wildest imagination—will abound throughout heaven. "But as it is written, Eye hath not seen, nor ear heard, neither have entered into the heart of man, the things which God hath prepared for them that love him" (1 Corinthians 2:9).

Need to Know
• John was a Jewish man. His visions were certainly influenced by the visions of the Old Testament prophets Isaiah and Ezekiel. The writings of these men also contain otherworldly visions of God with his angels (Isaiah 6:1–4; Ezekiel 1:4–21).
• Some see the creatures surrounding God as angelic beings of sort. Others see them as symbolic personifications of God's attributes: his all-knowing nature and his holiness.

Think About It
• Think about John's scenario of heavenly worship. Where do you see yourself in that scenario?
• How can we, through faith, accept the reality of a place and time that Scripture itself says we can't imagine?

Day 73

When I was a child, I spake as a child,
I understood as a child, I thought as a child:
but when I became a man, I put away childish things.
For now we see through a glass, darkly; but then face to face:
now I know in part; but then shall I know even as also I am known.
1 CORINTHIANS 13:11–12

After this I beheld, and, lo, a great multitude,
which no man could number, of all nations, and kindreds,
and people, and tongues, stood before the throne, and before the Lamb,
clothed with white robes, and palms in their hands;
And cried with a loud voice, saying,
Salvation to our God which sitteth upon the throne,
and unto the Lamb. And all the angels stood round about the throne,
and about the elders and the four beasts,
and fell before the throne on their faces, and worshipped God,
Saying, Amen: Blessing, and glory, and wisdom,
and thanksgiving, and honour, and power, and might,
be unto our God for ever and ever. Amen.
REVELATION 7:9–12

In His Presence

The Bible provides few glimpses of the believer's life in heaven. However, three themes dominate what we do know—worship, community, and service. They reflect God's original goal for humans before Adam and Eve's sin.

God created us to have a relationship with him (Genesis 1:26–27; 3:8). Throughout Revelation, heaven is portrayed as a place of unending praise for Jesus (Revelation 5:8–14; 7:9–17). We will no longer worship Jesus through the eyes of faith. Instead, we will see God's glory and will be filled with unspeakable joy (1 Corinthians 13:12; 2 Corinthians 5:7; 1 Peter 1:8; Revelation 22:3–4). God himself will illuminate the new Jerusalem, our eternal home, so that everyone will reflect the Lord's glory and be changed into his image (2 Corinthians 3:18; Revelation 21:23; 22:5).

Need to Know

- Throughout Scriptures, "seeing God" is represented as a potentially fatal endeavor. God hid Moses in the cleft of a mountain so that Moses wouldn't be completely exposed to God's face (Exodus 33:18–23). This gives some insight into the changes that will have taken place in heaven, where we will be in God's presence with no separation between us.
- Part of being in a relationship with God means being changed. The New Testament writers spoke often of our sanctification, the gradual molding to God's character revealed through Jesus (Romans 8:29). The reality of heaven will be that God will have completed that work in us.

Think About It

- How do you imagine your life in eternity?
- From what in this life do you most look forward to being redeemed?

DAY 74

Let not your heart be troubled:
ye believe in God, believe also in me.
In my Father's house are many mansions: if it were not so,
I would have told you. I go to prepare a place for you.
And if I go and prepare a place for you,
I will come again, and receive you unto myself;
that where I am, there ye may be also.
And whither I go ye know, and the way ye know.
Thomas saith unto him, Lord, we know not whither thou goest;
and how can we know the way? Jesus saith unto him,
I am the way, the truth, and the life: no man cometh unto the Father,
but by me. If ye had known me, ye should have known my Father also:
and from henceforth ye know him, and have seen him.

JOHN 14:1–7

WILL HEAVEN BE ALL IT'S CRACKED UP TO BE?

Most people have probably entertained, at least briefly, the possibility that heaven may not be the place of eternal happiness we're led to believe it is. Biblical depictions of worshiping and praising God for eternity do not necessarily coincide with our notions of enjoyable activities. Perhaps this is due to the fact that our attitudes concerning enjoyment and boredom are tainted by our limited earthly experiences. The truth is, we have absolutely no concept, no way of imagining, the pleasure and fulfillment that awaits us in heaven. Think of it this way: Not only is heaven a place prepared especially for us (John 14:2–4), it is also the place where God himself has chosen to dwell forever!

Need to Know

- It is difficult for us, bound in time that passes moment by moment, to imagine being in a realm in which time does not exist. We measure life's passing by the setting of the sun and the aging of our bodies. In the afterlife, those two things will not exist. We will be in a state of being with God, rather than a state of trying to get somewhere else.

- We think of heaven as the place where God dwells, but we must not forget that the work of Jesus paved the way for God's dwelling place to be within us. Heaven will be wonderful, but we don't have to wait for it to live in the presence of God now.

Think About It

- What kind of fulfillment do you expect in heaven that you haven't found in this life?
- How do your views of heaven differ today from your views as a child?

Day 75

But some man will say, How are the dead raised up?
and with what body do they come?
Thou fool, that which thou sowest is not quickened, except it die:
And that which thou sowest, thou sowest not that body that shall be,
but bare grain, it may chance of wheat, or of some other grain:
But God giveth it a body as it hath pleased him,
and to every seed his own body. All flesh is not the same flesh:
but there is one kind of flesh of men, another flesh of beasts,
another of fishes, and another of birds. There are also celestial bodies,
and bodies terrestrial: but the glory of the celestial is one,
and the glory of the terrestrial is another.
There is one glory of the sun, and another glory of the moon,
and another glory of the stars: for one star differeth from another star
in glory. So also is the resurrection of the dead.
It is sown in corruption; it is raised in incorruption:
It is sown in dishonour; it is raised in glory:
it is sown in weakness; it is raised in power:
It is sown a natural body; it is raised a spiritual body.
There is a natural body, and there is a spiritual body.
1 CORINTHIANS 15:35–44

Let us be glad and rejoice, and give honour to him:
for the marriage of the Lamb is come,
and his wife hath made herself ready.
And to her was granted that she should be arrayed in fine linen,
clean and white: for the fine linen is the righteousness of saints.
And he saith unto me, Write, Blessed are they which are called
unto the marriage supper of the Lamb.
And he saith unto me, These are the true sayings of God.
REVELATION 19:7–9

Let's Celebrate!

God's plan for people to exist in community (Genesis 1:27; 2:18) is fulfilled in heaven. One of Jesus' favorite metaphors to describe heaven is that of a wedding banquet, where everyone is eagerly welcomed and befriended (Matthew 22:2–14). Heaven will be a party that no one will want to leave. Revelation eagerly looks forward to this great wedding feast, which will celebrate the perfect union of Jesus and his church (Revelation 19:7–9). Believers are bound by such fellowship and love that together we are portrayed as Christ's bride. What an image of community!

In heaven, we will have glorified bodies (1 Corinthians 15:35–50). We will use these new bodies to serve God's kingdom. In a sense, God will be restoring us to our intended purpose, for he created Adam and Eve to serve him by cultivating the earth (Genesis 1:26, 28; Psalm 8:1–9). Jesus promises that we will be given authority to serve the kingdom in the future, even to reign as kings (Matthew 19:28–30; Revelation 2:26–27; 22:5). In the New Jerusalem, there will be new, exciting opportunities for learning, developing, and unfolding God's creation for his glory.

Need to Know
- The New Testament writers had just witnessed a change from an earthly body to a heavenly body—Jesus Christ. His body had changed enough that not everyone recognized him immediately, and he admonished Mary not to touch him (John 20:15–27). Yet he looked the same enough for them to eventually recognize who he was and relate to him as the Jesus they had known.
- When Jesus told the disciples that they would eventually rule with him, he made another wonderful promise as well. He promised that anyone who had given up anything because of their faith, would be paid back one hundred times the value of what they had lost (Matthew 19:29).

Think About It
- What do you see as your God-given responsibilities in this world to prepare for the next?

Day 76

And they say unto her, Woman, why weepest thou?
She saith unto them, Because they have taken away my Lord,
and I know not where they have laid him.
And when she had thus said, she turned herself back,
and saw Jesus standing, and knew not that it was Jesus.
Jesus saith unto her, Woman, why weepest thou? whom seekest thou?
She, supposing him to be the gardener, saith unto him,
Sir, if thou have borne him hence, tell me where thou hast laid him,
and I will take him away. Jesus saith unto her, Mary.
She turned herself, and saith unto him, Rabboni; which is to say,
Master. Jesus saith unto her, Touch me not;
for I am not yet ascended to my Father:
but go to my brethren, and say unto them,
I ascend unto my Father, and your Father;
and to my God, and your God.
Mary Magdalene came and told the disciples
that she had seen the Lord,
and that he had spoken these things unto her.
Then the same day at evening, being the first day of the week,
when the doors were shut where the disciples were assembled
for fear of the Jews, came Jesus and stood in the midst,
and saith unto them, Peace be unto you.
And when he had so said,
he shewed unto them his hands and his side.
Then were the disciples glad, when they saw the Lord.
Then said Jesus to them again, Peace be unto you:
as my Father hath sent me, even so send I you.
John 20:13–21

Will I Look Different in Heaven?

First, let's dispel some popular notions about our heavenly appearance and activity. Nowhere does Scripture describe citizens of heaven as sporting wings and halos, floating around on fluffy white clouds, or playing harps.

Contrary to another popular notion, we won't be mere spirits or ghosts in heaven. Jesus will raise our bodies from the dead and, after that, will determine our eternal destinies. At that time, we will have real, physical bodies, like that of the risen Christ. When Christ rose from the dead, he could eat. People even touched him (John 20–21). Yet his body was different somehow; it was transformed. This renewed, transformed body is what believers have to look forward to in heaven.

Need to Know
- Until he spoke her name, Mary Magdalene didn't recognize Jesus' transformed body after his resurrection. The two disciples on the road to Emmaus (Luke 24:15–16) also failed to recognize Jesus while they were with him, though they visited with him for quite some time.
- When Jesus appeared to the disciples, they thought him to be a spirit. He convinced them he was real by eating fish and honeycomb (Luke 24:33–41).

Think About It
- What are the popular notions you hear about heaven?
- One day God will transform your body. In what way, today, is he transforming your soul?

Day 77

And I saw thrones, and they sat upon them,
and judgment was given unto them:
and I saw the souls of them that were beheaded
for the witness of Jesus, and for the word of God,
and which had not worshipped the beast, neither his image,
neither had received his mark upon their foreheads, or in their hands;
and they lived and reigned with Christ a thousand years.
But the rest of the dead lived not again until
the thousand years were finished.
This is the first resurrection.
Blessed and holy is he that hath part in the first resurrection:
on such the second death hath no power,
but they shall be priests of God and of Christ,
and shall reign with him a thousand years.
REVELATION 20:4–6

And I saw the dead, small and great, stand before God;
and the books were opened: and another book was opened,
which is the book of life: and the dead were judged out of those things
which were written in the books, according to their works.
And the sea gave up the dead which were in it;
and death and hell delivered up the dead which were in them:
and they were judged every man according to their works.
REVELATION 20:12–13

USE WISDOM

Some people are hard to read. You can't tell when they're joking and when they're being serious. As a result, it's difficult to know when to accept their words at face value and when to take them with a grain of salt. The book of Revelation presents a similar problem. Bible scholars disagree as to how much of the book should be interpreted literally and how much should be viewed as symbolism. No passages in Revelation have inspired more controversy than those dealing with bodily resurrection (Revelation 20:4–6, 12–13).

We need to approach difficult texts like Revelation 20:4–6 with humility and caution. God's ways are above our own. But despite all the different interpretations of this passage, each end-times view confesses the return of Christ, a future bodily resurrection, a final judgment, and a new heaven and new earth. We know Jesus will one day return in glory to establish a better and perfect place.

Need to Know
- There are differing opinions of who is sitting on the thrones assisting in God's judgment. Some think they are the martyrs for the faith. Others think they are the twenty-four elders or even the twelve disciples. No one knows for sure.
- People who do not believe in a literal thousand-year reign interpret the first resurrection to be the spiritual resurrection we experience at the time of our salvation.

Think About It
- What is most important to you about Christ's return?
- What principles do you use to understand passages that people interpret many different ways?

Day 78

Now is the judgment of this world:
now shall the prince of this world be cast out.
JOHN 12:31

Knowing this, that our old man is crucified with him,
that the body of sin might be destroyed,
that henceforth we should not serve sin.
For he that is dead is freed from sin.
Now if we be dead with Christ,
we believe that we shall also live with him:
Knowing that Christ being raised from the dead dieth no more;
death hath no more dominion over him.
For in that he died, he died unto sin once:
but in that he liveth, he liveth unto God.
Likewise reckon ye also yourselves to be dead indeed unto sin,
but alive unto God through Jesus Christ our Lord.
ROMANS 6:6–11

And I saw an angel come down from heaven,
having the key of the bottomless pit and a great chain in his hand.
And he laid hold on the dragon, that old serpent, which is the Devil,
and Satan, and bound him a thousand years,
And cast him into the bottomless pit, and shut him up,
and set a seal upon him, that he should deceive the nations no more,
till the thousand years should be fulfilled:
and after that he must be loosed a little season.
REVELATION 20:1–3

Amillennialism: One Resurrection

Amillennialists believe in only one general resurrection at the end of this age. The book of Revelation, they observe, consists of visions that portray God's work throughout the entire church age. So Revelation 20:1–3 symbolically describes Jesus' binding of Satan during his earthly ministry (Matthew 12:29; John 12:31; Colossians 2:15). The Millennium, then, symbolizes the church age.

According to this view, the first resurrection, described in Revelation 20:6, refers to a person's salvation (Ezekiel 37:1–14; Romans 6:6–11; Ephesians 2:1, 5). Note that John refers to the "souls" of the martyrs, not their bodies (Revelation 20:4), suggesting a new spiritual existence. Revelation concludes that "the second death," or hell, "has no power over" those experiencing this first resurrection (Revelation 20:6; 21:8). The vision of the church age ends with a physical resurrection of all the dead for final judgment (Revelation 20:12–13).

Need to Know
- Resurrection has been a hot topic since the time of Christ, even before his resurrection. What set the Sadducees apart as religious leaders in Jesus' day was their doctrine that beyond death there is no resurrection.
- The church age refers to age in which we are living right now, as the church and body of Christ.

Think About It
- What seems most important to you about the final reign of Christ, even in the midst of so many differing opinions about the logistics of it?
- You are living in the church age. What do you think are the most significant contributions of the church in the present age?

DAY 79

And I saw thrones, and they sat upon them,
and judgment was given unto them:
and I saw the souls of them that were beheaded
for the witness of Jesus, and for the word of God,
and which had not worshipped the beast, neither his image,
neither had received his mark upon their foreheads, or in their hands;
and they lived and reigned with Christ a thousand years.
But the rest of the dead lived not again until the thousand years
were finished. This is the first resurrection. Blessed and holy is he that
hath part in the first resurrection: on such the second death hath no
power, but they shall be priests of God and of Christ, and shall reign
with him a thousand years. And when the thousand years are expired,
Satan shall be loosed out of his prison, And shall go out to deceive
the nations which are in the four quarters of the earth, Gog and Magog,
to gather them together to battle: the number of whom is as the
sand of the sea. And they went up on the breadth of the earth,
and compassed the camp of the saints about, and the beloved city:
and fire came down from God out of heaven, and devoured them.
And the devil that deceived them was cast into the lake of fire
and brimstone, where the beast and the false prophet are,
and shall be tormented day and night for ever and ever.

REVELATION 20:4–10

Postmillennialism: One Resurrection

Postmillennialists believe in a future age of spiritual prosperity for the church. They contend that the bodily resurrection for the righteous and the wicked occurs at Jesus' second coming.

Postmillennialists interpret the book of Revelation as a set of visions that reiterate God's work. They believe the final set of visions begins in Revelation 19:11 with the conquering Lamb slaying his enemies through the sword of his mouth. This supports their view that the Word of God will triumph over all opposition and establish a period of spiritual prosperity.

While the vision shifts in Revelation 20:4–6, the opening battle between God and Satan determines its context. John sees the raised souls of those who are martyred "for the witness of Jesus." Postmillennialists point out that while these souls reign with Christ, the text never states that Christ is present on earth. Postmillennialists interpret Revelation 20:4–6 as a vision of the Christian martyrs who are present with Christ in the "intermediate state." They are with Christ. They're rejoicing that Christ's cause has triumphed and that they won't go to hell (Philippians 1:23; Revelation 20:6; 21:8). So postmillennialists believe the second resurrection at the end of the Millennium is a physical resurrection of everyone to face God's final judgment.

Need to Know
- The "intermediate state" is the period of waiting for those who have died before the second coming and are yet to be resurrected with Christ. The parable of the rich man and Lazarus offers some foundation when interpreted literally (Luke 16:19–31).

Think About It
- Do you agree or disagree with the postmillennialist view?
- As you observe the points of your own faith, for what would you be willing to be martyred?

Day 80

And many of them that sleep in the dust of the earth shall awake,
some to everlasting life, and some to shame and everlasting contempt.
And they that be wise shall shine as the brightness of the firmament;
and they that turn many to righteousness as the stars for ever and ever.
But thou, O Daniel, shut up the words, and seal the book,
even to the time of the end: many shall run to and fro,
and knowledge shall be increased.

DANIEL 12:2–4

And Jesus answering said unto them,
The children of this world marry, and are given in marriage:
But they which shall be accounted worthy to obtain that world, and the
resurrection from the dead, neither marry, nor are given in marriage:
Neither can they die any more:
for they are equal unto the angels; and are the children of God,
being the children of the resurrection.
Now that the dead are raised, even Moses shewed at the bush,
when he calleth the Lord the God of Abraham,
and the God of Isaac, and the God of Jacob.
For he is not a God of the dead,
but of the living: for all live unto him.

LUKE 20:34–38

For if we believe that Jesus died and rose again,
even so them also which sleep in Jesus will God bring with him.
For this we say unto you by the word of the Lord,
that we which are alive and remain unto the coming of the Lord
shall not prevent them which are asleep.
For the Lord himself shall descend from heaven with a shout,
with the voice of the archangel, and with the trump of God:
and the dead in Christ shall rise first:
Then we which are alive and remain shall be caught up
together with them in the clouds, to meet the Lord in the air:
and so shall we ever be with the Lord.
Wherefore comfort one another with these words.
1 THESSALONIANS 4:14–18

Premillennialism: Two Resurrections

Premillennialists believe that Christ, at the Second Coming, resurrects dead believers to reign with him through the Millennium. After that, the rest of the dead are raised for the final judgment.

Premillennialists interpret Revelation 19:11–20:15 literally. In this vision of Armageddon, the conquering Lamb descends to earth and triumphs over his enemies (Revelation 19:13). Believers are raised to participate in Christ's reign on earth for one thousand years, after which the rest of the dead are raised.

Premillennialists point to Revelation 20:4–5 to support their belief in two bodily resurrections. The same Greek word *ezesan* ("lived" or "came back to life") is used to refer to the believers who come back to life before the Millennium and the remaining dead who return to life after the Millennium. Premillennialists point out that other Scripture passages suggest a two-stage bodily resurrection: first the righteous and then the wicked (Daniel 12:2; Luke 14:14; 20:35; 1 Thessalonians 4:16).

Need to Know

- In the premillennialist's view, there is a second and a third coming of Christ. In the second coming, Jesus secretly steals aways believers. Then, in the third, he returns in the sight of all to judge mankind.
- Jesus was resurrected to an eternal state. There were other resurrections in the Bible though—Lazarus (John 11), the daughter of Jairus (Luke 8) for instance—that were merely resurrections back to temporary life. There were also resurrections at the time of Jesus' resurrection. Matthew 27:50–53 tells us that many of the dead rose and appeared in the surrounding cities. All these people still faced eventual death.

Think About It

- How would you live your life differently were there no resurrection?
- How would you define the hope of the resurrection?

DAY 81

Then when Mary was come where Jesus was, and saw him,
she fell down at his feet, saying unto him,
Lord, if thou hadst been here, my brother had not died.
When Jesus therefore saw her weeping, and the Jews also weeping
which came with her, he groaned in the spirit, and was troubled,
And said, Where have ye laid him? They said unto him, Lord,
come and see. Jesus wept. Then said the Jews, Behold how he loved him!
And some of them said, Could not this man, which opened the eyes
of the blind, have caused that even this man should not have died?
Jesus therefore again groaning in himself cometh to the grave.
It was a cave, and a stone lay upon it. Jesus said, Take ye away
the stone. Martha, the sister of him that was dead, saith unto him,
Lord, by this time he stinketh: for he hath been dead four days.
Jesus saith unto her, Said I not unto thee, that,
if thou wouldest believe, thou shouldest see the glory of God?
Then they took away the stone from the place where the dead was laid.
And Jesus lifted up his eyes, and said, Father, I thank thee
that thou hast heard me. And I knew that thou hearest me always:
but because of the people which stand by I said it,
that they may believe that thou hast sent me.
And when he thus had spoken, he cried with a loud voice,
Lazarus, come forth. And he that was dead came forth,
bound hand and foot with graveclothes:
and his face was bound about with a napkin.
Jesus saith unto them, Loose him, and let him go.
JOHN 11:32–44

What Will Being Raised from the Dead Be Like?

The resurrection of believers is a physical, rather than merely a spiritual, event. The raising of Lazarus (John 11:38–44) and the Lord himself (Luke 24:36–39)—both of whom returned from the dead physically—serve as "previews" of the resurrection of believers.

The apostle Paul tells us that when Jesus returns, "the dead in Christ shall rise first" (1 Thessalonians 4:16). The event will be announced by the voice of the archangel and the blast of a trumpet. Immediately after the dead are raised, those believers who are still living will ascend to meet Jesus in the air (1 Thessalonians 4:17). What an exciting day that will be!

Need to Know
- Paul marks Christ's second coming with three signs: a shout, the call of the archangel, and the trumpet of God. These could be three distinct sounds or descriptions of the same sound.
- An archangel is an angel appointed to a certain task. If there is a developed hierarchy of angels, this would be an angel high in rank. Michael was called an archangel (Jude 9).

Think About It
- What do you believe about angels interacting with your everyday life?
- When you imagine suddenly hearing a sound that means the end has come, what do you think and feel?

TABLE: FAST FACTS ON ANGELS

Angels are mysterious beings. Their work is often "behind the scenes" and hidden from us. As servants of God, they carry out his will in this world. Many times, their task is to deliver messages to God's people. In the final days, angels will play a critical role in unleashing God's judgment on the world, but also in protecting God's people from harm.

Responsibility	Reference
Praise God, sing his infinite glory	Revelation 5:11–12
Provide aid to God's people in times of struggles	Psalm 91:9, 11; Hebrews 1:14
Help the church share the Good News of Christ	Revelation 14:6
Tell people God's coming judgment	Revelation 14:9–20
Accompany Jesus Christ at the Second Coming	2 Thessalonians 1:7–8
Directly influence the forces of nature	Revelation 7:1
Seal the 144,000 believing Israelites	Revelation 7:1–4
Pronounce the seven trumpet judgments	Revelation 8:2
Cast Satan and his angels out of heaven	Revelation 12:7–8
Announce the eternal hell awaiting unbelievers	Revelation 14:9–11
Predict and declare the fall of Babylon	Revelation 14:8; 18:1–2
Pour out the seven bowl judgments	Revelation 16:1
Announce Armageddon	Revelation 19:17–21
Chain Satan in the bottomless pit	Revelation 20:1–2
Carry out God's decision at the final judgment	Matthew 13:41–42, 49–50
Guard the new heaven and new earth	Revelation 21:12, 25, 27

DAY 82

*And there were in the same country shepherds abiding in the field,
keeping watch over their flock by night.
And, lo, the angel of the Lord came upon them,
and the glory of the Lord shone round about them:
and they were sore afraid. And the angel said unto them,
Fear not: for, behold, I bring you good tidings of great joy,
which shall be to all people. For unto you is born this day
in the city of David a Saviour, which is Christ the Lord.
And this shall be a sign unto you;
Ye shall find the babe wrapped in swaddling clothes, lying in a manger.
And suddenly there was with the angel a multitude of the heavenly host
praising God, and saying, Glory to God in the highest,
and on earth peace, good will toward men.*

LUKE 2:8–14

*And I beheld, and I heard the voice of many angels
round about the throne and the beasts and the elders: and
the number of them was ten thousand times ten thousand,
and thousands of thousands; Saying with a loud voice,
Worthy is the Lamb that was slain to receive power,
and riches, and wisdom, and strength,
and honour, and glory, and blessing.*

REVELATION 5:11–12

Angels

From television shows to greeting cards, angels have flown into our collective cultural heart. The yearning to be "touched by an angel" often reflects a desire to connect to some higher power or to "find one's self." But is that the purpose of angels? Do they exist simply to enhance our well-being?

Scripture tells us that angels are spiritual beings created by God to serve him in various capacities. As members of God's heavenly courts, angels number in the "thousands of thousands" (Revelation 5:11). When angels appear on earth, they often reflect their heavenly status through their dazzling radiance. Their appearance can terrify people (Luke 2:9; Revelation 4:5; 10:1).

Need to Know
- There are only two angels actually named in the Bible—Gabriel and Michael (and perhaps Satan, depending on how you view his origination).
- In the Old Testament, it is sometimes hard to tell whether an angel has appeared or a form of God himself, referred to as an "angel of the LORD."

Think About It
- Have you ever had an experience or heard of an experience that seemed to be somehow related to a modern-day interaction with an angel?
- Would you be terrified if an angel appeared to you with a message from God? What would it take to convince you it was really an angel from God?

Day 83

The LORD hath prepared his throne in the heavens;
and his kingdom ruleth over all. Bless the LORD, ye his angels,
that excel in strength, that do his commandments,
hearkening unto the voice of his word. Bless ye the LORD,
all ye his hosts; ye ministers of his, that do his pleasure.
Bless the LORD, all his works in all places of his dominion:
bless the LORD, O my soul.
PSALM 103:19–22

Praise ye the LORD.
Praise ye the LORD from the heavens:
praise him in the heights.
Praise ye him, all his angels:
praise ye him, all his hosts.
Praise ye him, sun and moon:
praise him, all ye stars of light.
Praise him, ye heavens of heavens,
and ye waters that be above the heavens.
Let them praise the name of the LORD:
for he commanded, and they were created.
PSALM 148:1–5

What Angels Do

The primary task of angels is to praise God (Psalm 103:20; 148:1–2; Daniel 7:10). The sheer number and awesome worship of the angelic host affirm God's infinite glory (Isaiah 6:3; Revelation 5:11–13). In heaven Satan coveted this type of worship for himself, and his rebellion led other angels to fall as well. So now angels are divided into two groups: the righteous and the wicked. The wicked angels, demons, were defeated when Jesus died on the cross. God will eventually condemn them to the lake of fire (Matthew 25:41; Colossians 2:15). The righteous angels, on the other hand, are instrumental in God's battle against evil.

Need to Know
- Angels—righteous and wicked—are created beings with limitations. They are neither omniscient nor omnipresent.
- Each of the seven churches addressed in the first three chapters of Revelation was addressed through an angel. There are a variety of interpretations of the identity of these angels.

Think About It
- Given the choice of whether to be an angel of God or a redeemed child of God, which would you choose?
- The primary task of angels is to praise God. How would you define your primary task before God?

Day 84

Then saith Jesus unto him, Get thee hence,
Satan: for it is written,
Thou shalt worship the Lord thy God,
and him only shalt thou serve.
Then the devil leaveth him, and, behold,
angels came and ministered unto him.
MATTHEW 4:10–11

And, behold, there was a great earthquake:
for the angel of the Lord descended from heaven,
and came and rolled back the stone from the door, and sat upon it.
His countenance was like lightning, and his raiment white as snow:
And for fear of him the keepers did shake, and became as dead men.
And the angel answered and said unto the women,
Fear not ye: for I know that ye seek Jesus, which was crucified.
He is not here: for he is risen, as he said. Come, see the place where the
Lord lay. And go quickly, and tell his disciples that he is risen
from the dead; and, behold, he goeth before you into Galilee;
there shall ye see him: lo, I have told you.
MATTHEW 28:2–7

But the angel of the Lord by night opened the prison doors,
and brought them forth, and said,
Go, stand and speak in the temple to the people all the words of this life.
ACTS 5:19–20

Angels Do God's Work

Angels not only announced the birth of the Messiah (Luke 1:5–38; 2:8–20), they were also the first to proclaim Jesus' victory over death (Matthew 28:2–7). They prodded the church to spread the Good News of Christ to non-Jews and the leaders of the world (Acts 5:19; 8:26; 10:3–8, 22; 27:23–24). Revelation suggests this same role for angels in the end times. Angels are responsible for leading the church to proclaim the Good News "to every nation, and kindred, and tongue, and people" (Revelation 10:7; 14:6–7, 9–11).

Angels ministered to Jesus throughout his time on earth, particularly during such difficult circumstances as his temptation and his moment of decision in Gethsemane (Matthew 4:11; Mark 1:13; Luke 22:43). The angels provided strength for Jesus, bringing him food during the forty days of his temptation and spiritually comforting him. Scripture promises that angels will help believers as well (Hebrews 1:14). In Revelation, the angels of the seven churches fulfill this role by communicating God's praise as well as God's rebuke to believers (Revelation 2:1–3:22).

Need to Know
- In the Bible, angels typically appeared familiar enough to be accepted by people, but different enough—extremely white or light—to give them credence as creatures outside of this world (Matthew 28:3).
- Angelology is the doctrine of angels. Angels are not of major study in Christian theology, but recognized as playing a role in much of God's work throughout human history. Paul warned the Colossian Christians to refrain from worshiping angels (Colossians 2:18–19).

Think About It
- If you could ask an angel any question, what would it be?
- What message do you need to receive from God in this season of your life?

Day 85

He answered and said unto them,
He that soweth the good seed is the Son of man;
The field is the world; the good seed are the children of the kingdom;
but the tares are the children of the wicked one;
The enemy that sowed them is the devil;
the harvest is the end of the world; and the reapers are the angels.
As therefore the tares are gathered and burned in the fire;
so shall it be in the end of this world.
The Son of man shall send forth his angels,
and they shall gather out of his kingdom all things that offend,
and them which do iniquity; and shall cast them into a furnace of fire:
there shall be wailing and gnashing of teeth.
Then shall the righteous shine forth as the sun
in the kingdom of their Father.
Who hath ears to hear, let him hear.
MATTHEW 13:37–43

Again, the kingdom of heaven is like unto a net,
that was cast into the sea, and gathered of every kind:
Which, when it was full, they drew to shore, and sat down,
and gathered the good into vessels, but cast the bad away.
So shall it be at the end of the world: the angels shall come forth,
and sever the wicked from among the just,
and shall cast them into the furnace of fire:
there shall be wailing and gnashing of teeth.
Jesus saith unto them,
Have ye understood all these things?
They say unto him, Yea, Lord.
MATTHEW 13:47–51

ANGELS OF WRATH

Jesus promised that angels would accompany him at the Second Coming and help separate the wicked from the righteous at the final judgment (Matthew 13:41, 49; 25:31; Mark 8:38). Revelation details this role of angels as the emissaries of the conquering Lamb's judgment. When the Lamb opens the seals to unleash God's wrath on the wicked (Revelation 5—6), the angels typically summon these judgments and often personally carry them out (Revelation 6:1–7; 7:2–3; 14:14–20; 16:1–21; 20:1–3). For instance, the seventh angel pours out the vial of God's fierce anger on Babylon, producing an earthquake that causes mountains to dissolve and the city to be "divided into three parts" (Revelation 16:17–20).

Need to Know
- The seals were attached to scrolls. An angel asked, Who could open the scrolls by breaking the seals? Jesus, the Lamb, was the only one worthy.
- The vials, or bowls, of judgment and their resulting plagues came on the heels of other judgments. First, the plagues from the seals destroyed a fourth of the earth. Then the trumpets brought judgments that destroyed another third of the earth. The seven bowls (vials), poured by seven angels, were directed toward the antichrist's followers but also affected what remained of the earth.

Think About It
- The seals, the trumpets, and the bowls—all symbols of judgment. What best symbolizes God's judgment in your life?
- How much of your initiative in obeying God is prompted by judgment?

TABLE: FAST FACTS ON THE SEVEN BOWL JUDGMENTS

Seven bowls (vials) of God's wrath are poured out upon the earth after the seven seal judgments and seven trumpet judgments. These bowls represent God's final pronouncements against the earth. The plagues that result will devastate the human race and prepare it for Jesus' arrival.

Bowl	Judgment	Results	Reference
First bowl	Horribly painful sores break out on people who have submitted to the beast.	These sores will cause agonizing pain for the unrepentant.	Revelation 16:2
Second bowl	The sea turns into blood, and all aquatic life dies.	When the sea dies, the fate of the world is set.	Revelation 16:3
Third bowl	The water in springs and rivers turns into blood.	With the fresh water polluted, life on earth becomes very precarious.	Revelation 16:4
Fourth bowl	The sun is allowed to severely burn people.	People remain rooted in their fierce rejection of and hatred for God.	Revelation 16:8

Bowl	Judgment	Results	Reference
Fifth bowl	Darkness covers the earth.	Under the cover of darkness, unrepentant people continue to cry out against God.	Revelation 16:10
Sixth bowl	The great Euphrates River dries up.	This disaster creates the pathway for the gathering of the armies of Armageddon.	Revelation 16:12
Seventh bowl	A devastating earthquake, accompanied by hail, alters the surface of the earth.	Great cities collapse and people harden their hearts in their hatred for God.	Revelation 16:17–21

Day 86

That the God of our Lord Jesus Christ, the Father of glory,
may give unto you the spirit of wisdom and revelation
in the knowledge of him:
The eyes of your understanding being enlightened;
that ye may know what is the hope of his calling,
and what the riches of the glory of his inheritance in the saints,
And what is the exceeding greatness of his power to us-ward who believe,
according to the working of his mighty power,
which he wrought in Christ, when he raised him from the dead,
and set him at his own right hand in the heavenly places,
Far above all principality, and power, and might, and dominion,
and every name that is named, not only in this world,
but also in that which is to come:
And hath put all things under his feet,
and gave him to be the head over all things to the church,
which is his body, the fulness of him that filleth all in all.
EPHESIANS 1:17–23

Let no man therefore judge you in meat, or in drink,
or in respect of an holyday, or of the new moon, or of the sabbath days:
which are a shadow of things to come; but the body is of Christ.
Let no man beguile you of your reward in a voluntary humility
and worshipping of angels, intruding into those things which he hath
not seen, vainly puffed up by his fleshly mind, and not holding the Head,
from which all the body by joints and bands having nourishment
ministered, and knit together, increaseth with the increase of God.
COLOSSIANS 2:16–19

For Christ also hath once suffered for sins,
the just for the unjust, that he might bring us to God,
being put to death in the flesh, but quickened by the Spirit:
by which also he went and preached unto the spirits in prison;
which sometime were disobedient, when once the longsuffering of God
waited in the days of Noah, while the ark was a preparing,
wherein few, that is, eight souls were saved by water.
The like figure whereunto even baptism doth also now save us
(not the putting away of the filth of the flesh,
but the answer of a good conscience toward God,)
by the resurrection of Jesus Christ: who is gone into heaven,
and is on the right hand of God; angels and authorities
and powers being made subject unto him.
1 PETER 3:18–22

Under Jesus' Command

While angels are an integral part of Scripture's vision of the end times, they always serve Jesus. Angels had absolutely no part in saving us. Revelation's account of the warfare between God's angels and Satan does not suggest that the angels achieve victory on their own. Rather, Satan isn't strong enough to defeat the angels because of the "blood of the lamb" (Revelation 12:11). The angels do fight Satan and his demons (Daniel 10:10–13; Revelation 12:7–12), but Christ directs the battle and delivered that final, defeating blow to Satan when he died on the cross. So the angels are more like privates in Jesus' heavenly army. They're more like ringside attendants at a boxing match. They remove the defeated from the ring. Jesus alone is the conquering Lamb. Jesus alone defeats Satan once and for all!

Jesus is supreme over all angelic beings. The angels were created to serve him (Ephesians 1:20–22; 1 Peter 3:22). Any angel who diverts attention from Jesus belongs to Satan's camp, for Jesus alone should receive our worship (Colossians 2:18; Revelation 22:8–9). We must not let our culture's fascination with angels divert our attention from the only one who can save: Jesus Christ!

Need to Know
- Angels do not marry and do not die (Luke 20:34–36). They are not a race descended from others, but rather a group created by God, probably genderless.
- At Jesus' ascension it was two angels who announced to the crowd that Jesus would return the same way (Acts 1:10–11).

Think About It
- Besides angels, what else does our culture focus on rather than Jesus for the source of spirituality?
- What things in your life function as rivals for Christ's supremacy?

Day 87

Beware of false prophets, which come to you in sheep's clothing,
but inwardly they are ravening wolves.
Ye shall know them by their fruits.
Do men gather grapes of thorns, or figs of thistles?
Even so every good tree bringeth forth good fruit;
but a corrupt tree bringeth forth evil fruit.
A good tree cannot bring forth evil fruit,
neither can a corrupt tree bring forth good fruit.
Every tree that bringeth not forth good fruit is hewn down,
and cast into the fire.
Wherefore by their fruits ye shall know them.
MATTHEW 7:15–20

Be not deceived; God is not mocked:
for whatsoever a man soweth, that shall he also reap.
For he that soweth to his flesh shall of the flesh reap corruption;
but he that soweth to the Spirit shall of the Spirit reap life everlasting.
And let us not be weary in well doing: for in due season we shall reap,
if we faint not. As we have therefore opportunity, let us do good
unto all men, especially unto them who are of the household of faith.
GALATIANS 6:7–10

Rewards

Scripture promises that Christ will judge all people on the basis of their works at the final judgment. Even the judgment of believers will focus on works because our faith must be active in forgiveness, in love, and in good works. After all, a good tree bears good fruit (Matthew 7:17–19; Galatians 5:6; James 2:26). Scripture promises not only that God has saved us for good works, but also that he will reward whatever good we do (see Ephesians 6:8; 1 Corinthians 3:11–15; 9:16–27; 2 Corinthians 5:10; Galatians 6:7–10; Ephesians 2:10; 1 Peter 5:1–4).

Need to Know
- We think of being rewarded for something good and punished for something bad. The word *reward* actually applies to both. You will receive the appropriate reward for your actions, whether it is positive or negative.
- The writer of Ecclesiastes noted that we can't expect rewards in this life. Sometimes in this life the righteous suffer and the wicked prosper. We must trust God to reward our faith in his time (Ecclesiastes 7:14–17).

Think About It
- What kind of spiritual fruit does your life bear?
- As you evaluate your own life, do good works pour out of your sincere faith?

TABLE: VICTORY PRIZES

Everyone wants to win—whether it's a race, a game, or even in one's career. Jesus, in the book of Revelation, challenges us to be winners and overcomers in the Christian life and to remain true to him in the face of difficulty, temptation, and suffering. (Revelation 2:11; 3:12; 21:7). Those who overcome evil in this life with God's help will reap a harvest of eternal treasures.

Promise	Reference
Jesus will give the victors the right to eat from the tree of life	Revelation 2:7
Those who win the victory will not be hurt by the second death	Revelation 2:11
Jesus will give them hidden manna	Revelation 2:17
Jesus will give each victor a white stone with a new name written on it	Revelation 2:17
Jesus will give the victors authority over the nations	Revelation 2:26
Those who win the victory will be dressed in white	Revelation 3:5
The victors will have their names inscribed in the Book of Life, and Jesus will acknowledge them before his Father and the angels	Revelation 3:5
Those who win the victory will be like pillars in the temple of God	Revelation 3:12
The victors will wear God's name, the name of the new Jerusalem, and Jesus' new name	Revelation 3:12
Jesus will give them the right to sit with him on his throne	Revelation 3:21
Everyone who wins the victory will inherit the new heaven and new earth	Revelation 21:7

DAY 88

Take heed that ye do not your alms before men, to be seen of them:
otherwise ye have no reward of your Father which is in heaven.
Therefore when thou doest thine alms,
do not sound a trumpet
before thee, as the hypocrites do in the synagogues and in the streets,
that they may have glory of men.
Verily I say unto you, They have their reward.
But when thou doest alms,
let not thy left hand know what thy right hand doeth:
That thine alms may be in secret:
and thy Father which seeth in secret himself
shall reward thee openly.
MATTHEW 6:1–4

For other foundation can no man lay than that is laid,
which is Jesus Christ.
Now if any man build upon this foundation gold,
silver, precious stones, wood, hay, stubble;
Every man's work shall be made manifest:
for the day shall declare it, because it shall be revealed by fire;
and the fire shall try every man's work of what sort it is.
If any man's work abide which he hath built thereupon,
he shall receive a reward. If any man's work shall be burned,
he shall suffer loss: but he himself shall be saved; yet so as by fire.
Know ye not that ye are the temple of God, and that the Spirit of God
dwelleth in you? If any man defile the temple of God,
him shall God destroy; for the temple of God is holy,
which temple ye are.
1 CORINTHIANS 3:11–17

Paul's Teaching on Rewards

The apostle Paul explained the concept of rewards in more detail. While he emphatically affirms that Christ is the only foundation for our salvation, various structures can be erected on that foundation. Some structures are made of gold and precious stones; others are made of hay and straw. On the day of judgment, these structures will be tested by fire. "If any man's work abide which he hath built thereupon, he shall receive a reward. If any man's work shall be burned, he shall suffer loss" (1 Corinthians 3:14–15). This does not imply damnation, because the person "shall be saved; yet so as by fire" (1 Corinthians 3:15). Both builders are saved, but only the one whose building survives receives a reward. If the motive for one's works is self-glory and not the glory of God, the result is loss. Likewise, if one's motive is seeking the praise of people, there will be no reward from God (Matthew 6:1).

Need to Know
- Jesus told the story of a man who built his house on rock and one who built his house on sand. When the storms came, the house built on rock was the only one that withstood (Matthew 7:24–27). Often our rewards are the consequences of our actions.
- Another way to look at rewards is sowing and reaping. This concept is woven throughout Scripture, from Job's friend Eliphaz (Job 4:8), to the writer of the Proverbs (Proverbs 22:8), to Paul the apostle (2 Corinthians 9:6).

Think About It
- What are you sowing spiritually, and what will you reap from it?
- What reward do you think you'll receive from God?

Day 89

But we all, with open face beholding as in a glass
the glory of the Lord, are changed into the same image
from glory to glory, even as by the Spirit of the Lord.
2 Corinthians 3:18

For we are his workmanship,
created in Christ Jesus unto good works,
which God hath before ordained that we should walk in them.
Ephesians 2:10

I have fought a good fight, I have finished my course,
I have kept the faith:
Henceforth there is laid up for me a crown of righteousness,
which the Lord, the righteous judge, shall give me at that day:
and not to me only, but unto all them also that love his appearing.
2 Timothy 4:7–8

Behold, I come quickly: hold that fast which thou hast,
that no man take thy crown.
Revelation 3:11

Why Are Crowns Important?

What are these rewards that the Bible depicts as crowns (1 Corinthians 9:25; Revelation 2:10; 3:11)? Scripture describes them simply as the virtues of being like Christ. The "crown of glory that fadeth not away" (1 Peter 5:4) refers to the fact that we will reflect Christ's own image of God's glory (2 Corinthians 3:18). The crown of righteousness (2 Timothy 4:8) refers to Christ's righteousness, which we will embody in the future (Romans 8:3–4; Ephesians 2:10). The prize of rejoicing in other believers (Philippians 4:1; 1 Thessalonians 2:19) reflects Christ's kingdom of reconciling love. The eternal "crown of life" (James 1:12; Revelation 2:10) refers to communion with Christ forever. In other words, these prizes are the characteristics of the Christian life.

Need to Know
- In the Old Testament crowns symbolized a specialty or specialized task. Priests wore crowns marked, "holy to the Lord." Hebrew kings wore simple crowns that could be worn into battle. Wreaths of flowers were also worn as crowns in celebrations.
- Jesus' crown of thorns was a parody of a victor's wreath—a laurel wreath worn as an honor—used to shame and disdain him.

Think About It
- How do you respond to the idea that our crowns will be our Christlikeness?
- In what ways can you see that God is making you like Christ?

Day 90

He said therefore,
A certain nobleman went into a far country
to receive for himself a kingdom, and to return.
And he called his ten servants, and delivered them ten pounds,
and said unto them, Occupy till I come.
But his citizens hated him, and sent a message after him, saying,
We will not have this man to reign over us.
And it came to pass, that when he was returned,
having received the kingdom, then he commanded these servants
to be called unto him, to whom he had given the money,
that he might know how much every man had gained by trading.
Then came the first, saying, Lord, thy pound hath gained ten pounds.
And he said unto him,
Well, thou good servant: because thou hast been faithful in a very little,
have thou authority over ten cities. And the second came, saying, Lord,
thy pound hath gained five pounds. And he said likewise to him,
Be thou also over five cities. And another came, saying,
Lord, behold, here is thy pound,
which I have kept laid up in a napkin: For I feared thee,
because thou art an austere man:
thou takest up that thou layedst not down,
and reapest that thou didst not sow.
And he saith unto him,
Out of thine own mouth will I judge thee, thou wicked servant.
Thou knewest that I was an austere man, taking up that I laid not
down, and reaping that I did not sow:
Wherefore then gavest not thou my money into the bank,
that at my coming I might have required mine own with usury?
And he said unto them that stood by,
Take from him the pound, and give it to him that hath ten pounds.
LUKE 19:12–24

The four and twenty elders fall down
before him that sat on the throne,
and worship him that liveth for ever and ever,
and cast their crowns before the throne, saying,
Thou art worthy, O Lord, to receive glory and honour
and power: for thou hast created all things,
and for thy pleasure they are and were created.
REVELATION 4:10–11

Rewarded According to Our Works

Many premillennialists also connect these rewards with reigning in Christ's millennial kingdom (Luke 22:30; 1 Corinthians 6:2–3; 2 Timothy 2:12; Revelation 20:4). Several of Jesus' parables suggest that he will offer the reward of ruling to the faithful when he returns (Matthew 25:14–30; Luke 19:12–27). Amillennialists interpret this reward as increased responsibility in the new earth (Revelation 5:9–10), new opportunities for learning and cultivating God's creation for his glory.

Believers will be rewarded for their good works at the day of judgment. But by their very nature, these crowns nurture and intensify our attempts to be like Christ. These rewards won't bring attention to the person who receives it, but will ultimately bring glory to God. Like the white-robed leaders described in Revelation 4:10, believers will cast their crowns before Christ, praising God, "Thou art worthy, O Lord, to receive glory and honour and power" (Revelation 4:11).

Need to Know

- In the parable of Luke 19, the nobleman left for a time. If Jesus represents the nobleman in the parable, which most agree he does, then the story makes the point that Jesus will be gone for a time, leaving the world in our hands to run it well.
- The Greek word used here for *crowns* denotes a victor's crown or honor for distinguished service. Any and all honor we receive from God will be offered back to him who is worthy of all praise.

Think About It

- How do you use the resources God's given you by investing them wisely?
- How would you like to be living differently in light of the reality that you will stand before God one day?

NOTES

NOTES

Notes

NOTES

Bible Readings for January

January 1 - LUKE 5:27–39, GENESIS 1–2, PSALM 1
January 2 - LUKE 6:1–26, GENESIS 3–5, PSALM 2
January 3 - LUKE 6:27–49, GENESIS 6–7, PSALM 3
January 4 - LUKE 7:1–17, GENESIS 8–10, PSALM 4
January 5 - LUKE 7:18–50, GENESIS 11, PSALM 5
January 6 - LUKE 8:1–25, GENESIS 12, PSALM 6
January 7 - LUKE 8:26–56, GENESIS 13–14, PSALM 7
January 8 - LUKE 9:1–27, GENESIS 15, PSALM 8
January 9 - LUKE 9:28–62, GENESIS 16, PSALM 9
January 10 - LUKE 10:1–20, GENESIS 17, PSALM 10
January 11 - LUKE 10:21–42, GENESIS 18, PSALM 11
January 12 - LUKE 11:1–28, GENESIS 19, PSALM 12
January 13 - LUKE 11:29–54, GENESIS 20, PSALM 13
January 14 - LUKE 12:1–31, GENESIS 21, PSALM 14
January 15 - LUKE 12:32–59, GENESIS 22, PSALM 15
January 16 - LUKE 13:1–17, GENESIS 23, PSALM 16
January 17 - LUKE 13:18–35, GENESIS 24, PSALM 17
January 18 - LUKE 14:1–24, GENESIS 25, PSALM 18
January 19 - LUKE 14:25–35, GENESIS 26, PSALM 19
January 20 - LUKE 15, GENESIS 27:1–45, PSALM 20
January 21 - LUKE 16, GENESIS 27:46–28:22, PSALM 21
January 22 - LUKE 17, GENESIS 29:1–30, PSALM 22
January 23 - LUKE 18:1–17, GENESIS 29:31–30:43, PSALM 23
January 24 - LUKE 18:18–43, GENESIS 31, PSALM 24
January 25 - LUKE 19:1–27, GENESIS 32–33, PSALM 25
January 26 - LUKE 19:28–48, GENESIS 34, PSALM 26
January 27 - LUKE 20:1–26, GENESIS 35–36, PSALM 27
January 28 - LUKE 20:27–47, GENESIS 37, PSALM 28
January 29 - LUKE 21, GENESIS 38, PSALM 29
January 30 - LUKE 22:1–38, GENESIS 39, PSALM 30
January 31 - LUKE 22:39–71, GENESIS 40, PSALM 31

Bible Readings for February

February 1 - LUKE 23:1–25, GENESIS 41, PSALM 32
February 2 - LUKE 23:26–56, GENESIS 42, PSALM 33
February 3 - LUKE 24:1–12, GENESIS 43, PSALM 34
February 4 - LUKE 24:13–53, GENESIS 44, PSALM 35
February 5 - HEBREWS 1, GENESIS 45:1–46:27, PSALM 36
February 6 - HEBREWS 2, GENESIS 46:28–47:31, PSALM 37
February 7 - HEBREWS 3:1–4:13, GENESIS 48, PSALM 38
February 8 - HEBREWS 4:14–6:12, GENESIS 49–50, PSALM 39
February 9 - HEBREWS 6:13–20, EXODUS 1–2, PSALM 40
February 10 - HEBREWS 7, EXODUS 3–4, PSALM 41
February 11 - HEBREWS 8, EXODUS 5:1–6:27, PROVERBS 1
February 12 - HEBREWS 9:1–22, EXODUS 6:28–8:32, PROVERBS 2
February 13 - HEBREWS 9:23–10:18, EXODUS 9–10, PROVERBS 3
February 14 - HEBREWS 10:19–39, EXODUS 11–12, PROVERBS 4
February 15 - HEBREWS 11:1–22, EXODUS 13–14, PROVERBS 5
February 16 - HEBREWS 11:23–40, EXODUS 15, PROVERBS 6:1–7:5
February 17 - HEBREWS 12, EXODUS 16–17, PROVERBS 7:6–27
February 18 - HEBREWS 13, EXODUS 18–19, PROVERBS 8
February 19 - MATTHEW 1, EXODUS 20–21, PROVERBS 9
February 20 - MATTHEW 2, EXODUS 22–23, PROVERBS 10
February 21 - MATTHEW 3, EXODUS 24, PROVERBS 11
February 22 - MATTHEW 4, EXODUS 25–27, PROVERBS 12
February 23 - MATTHEW 5:1–20, EXODUS 28–29, PROVERBS 13
February 24 - MATTHEW 5:21–48, EXODUS 30–32, PROVERBS 14
February 25 - MATTHEW 6:1–18, EXODUS 33–34, PROVERBS 15
February 26 - MATTHEW 6:19–34, EXODUS 35–36, PROVERBS 16
February 27 - MATTHEW 7, EXODUS 37–38, PROVERBS 17
February 28 - MATTHEW 8:1–13, EXODUS 39–40, PROVERBS 18

BIBLE READINGS FOR MARCH

March 1 - MATTHEW 8:14–34, LEVITICUS 1–2, PROVERBS 19
March 2 - MATTHEW 9:1–17, LEVITICUS 3–4, PROVERBS 20
March 3 - MATTHEW 9:18–38, LEVITICUS 5–6, PROVERBS 21
March 4 - MATTHEW 10:1–25, LEVITICUS 7–8, PROVERBS 22
March 5 - MATTHEW 10:26–42, LEVITICUS 9–10, PROVERBS 23
March 6 - MATTHEW 11:1–19, LEVITICUS 11–12, PROVERBS 24
March 7 - MATTHEW 11:20–30, LEVITICUS 13, PROVERBS 25
March 8 - MATTHEW 12:1–21, LEVITICUS 14, PROVERBS 26
March 9 - MATTHEW 12:22–50, LEVITICUS 15–16, PROVERBS 27
March 10 - MATTHEW 13:1–23, LEVITICUS 17–18, PROVERBS 28
March 11 - MATTHEW 13:24–58, LEVITICUS 19, PROVERBS 29
March 12 - MATTHEW 14:1–21, LEVITICUS 20–21, PROVERBS 30
March 13 - MATTHEW 14:22–36, LEVITICUS 22–23, PROVERBS 31
March 14 - MATTHEW 15:1–20, LEVITICUS 24–25, ECCLESIASTES 1:1–11
March 15 - MATTHEW 15:21–39, LEVITICUS 26–27, ECCLESIASTES
        1:12–2:26
March 16 - MATTHEW 16, NUMBERS 1–2, ECCLESIASTES 3:1–15
March 17 - MATTHEW 17, NUMBERS 3–4, ECCLESIASTES 3:16–4:16
March 18 - MATTHEW 18:1–20, NUMBERS 5–6, ECCLESIASTES 5
March 19 - MATTHEW 18:21–35, NUMBERS 7–8, ECCLESIASTES 6
March 20 - MATTHEW 19:1–15, NUMBERS 9–10, ECCLESIASTES 7
March 21 - MATTHEW 19:16–30, NUMBERS 11–12, ECCLESIASTES 8
March 22 - MATTHEW 20:1–16, NUMBERS 13–14, ECCLESIASTES
        9:1–12
March 23 - MATTHEW 20:17–34, NUMBERS 15–16, ECCLESIASTES
        9:13–10:20
March 24 - MATTHEW 21:1–27, NUMBERS 17–18, ECCLESIASTES
        11:1–8
March 25 - MATTHEW 21:28–46, NUMBERS 19–20, ECCLESIASTES
        11:9–12:14
March 26 - MATTHEW 22:1–22, NUMBERS 21, SONG OF SOLOMON
        1:1–2:7

BIBLE READINGS FOR APRIL

April 1 - MATTHEW 25:1–30, NUMBERS 30–31, JOB 1
April 2 - MATTHEW 25:31–46, NUMBERS 32–34, JOB 2
April 3 - MATTHEW 26:1–25, NUMBERS 35–36, JOB 3
April 4 - MATTHEW 26:26–46, DEUTERONOMY 1–2, JOB 4
April 5 - MATTHEW 26:47–75, DEUTERONOMY 3–4, JOB 5
April 6 - MATTHEW 27:1–31, DEUTERONOMY 5–6, JOB 6
April 7 - MATTHEW 27:32–66, DEUTERONOMY 7–8, JOB 7
April 8 - MATTHEW 28, DEUTERONOMY 9–10, JOB 8
April 9 - ACTS 1, DEUTERONOMY 11–12, JOB 9
April 10 - ACTS 2:1–13, DEUTERONOMY 13–14, JOB 10
April 11 - ACTS 2:14–47, DEUTERONOMY 15–16, JOB 11
April 12 - ACTS 3, DEUTERONOMY 17–18, JOB 12
April 13 - ACTS 4:1–22, DEUTERONOMY 19–20, JOB 13
April 14 - ACTS 4:23–37, DEUTERONOMY 21–22, JOB 14
April 15 - ACTS 5:1–16, DEUTERONOMY 23–24, JOB 15
April 16 - ACTS 5:17–42, DEUTERONOMY 25–27, JOB 16
April 17 - ACTS 6, DEUTERONOMY 28, JOB 17
April 18 - ACTS 7:1–22, DEUTERONOMY 29–30, JOB 18
April 19 - ACTS 7:23–60, DEUTERONOMY 31–32, JOB 19
April 20 - ACTS 8:1–25, DEUTERONOMY 33–34, JOB 20
April 21 - ACTS 8:26–40, JOSHUA 1–2, JOB 21
April 22 - ACTS 9:1–25, JOSHUA 3:1–5:1, JOB 22
April 23 - ACTS 9:26–43, JOSHUA 5:2–6:27, JOB 23
April 24 - ACTS 10:1–33, JOSHUA 7–8, JOB 24
April 25 - ACTS 10:34–48, JOSHUA 9–10, JOB 25
April 26 - ACTS 11:1–18, JOSHUA 11–12, JOB 26
April 27 - ACTS 11:19–30, JOSHUA 13–14, JOB 27
April 28 - ACTS 12, JOSHUA 15–17, JOB 28
April 29 - ACTS 13:1–25, JOSHUA 18–19, JOB 29
April 30 - ACTS 13:26–52, JOSHUA 20–21, JOB 30

Bible Readings for May

May 1 - Acts 14, Joshua 22, Job 31
May 2 - Acts 15:1–21, Joshua 23–24, Job 32
May 3 - Acts 15:22–41, Judges 1, Job 33
May 4 - Acts 16:1–15, Judges 2–3, Job 34
May 5 - Acts 16:16–40, Judges 4–5, Job 35
May 6 - Acts 17:1–15, Judges 6, Job 36
May 7 - Acts 17:16–34, Judges 7–8, Job 37
May 8 - Acts 18, Judges 9, Job 38
May 9 - Acts 19:1–20, Judges 10:1–11:33, Job 39
May 10 - Acts 19:21–41, Judges 11:34–12:15, Job 40
May 11 - Acts 20:1–16, Judges 13, Job 41
May 12 - Acts 20:17–38, Judges 14–15, Job 42
May 13 - Acts 21:1–36, Judges 16, Psalm 42
May 14 - Acts 21:37–22:29, Judges 17–18, Psalm 43
May 15 - Acts 22:30–23:22, Judges 19, Psalm 44
May 16 - Acts 23:23–24:9, Judges 20, Psalm 45
May 17 - Acts 24:10–27, Judges 21, Psalm 46
May 18 - Acts 25, Ruth 1–2, Psalm 47
May 19 - Acts 26:1–18, Ruth 3–4, Psalm 48
May 20 - Acts 26:19–32, 1 Samuel 1:1–2:10, Psalm 49
May 21 - Acts 27:1–12, 1 Samuel 2:11–36, Psalm 50
May 22 - Acts 27:13–44, 1 Samuel 3, Psalm 51
May 23 - Acts 28:1–16, 1 Samuel 4–5, Psalm 52
May 24 - Acts 28:17–31, 1 Samuel 6–7, Psalm 53
May 25 - Romans 1:1–15, 1 Samuel 8, Psalm 54
May 26 - Romans 1:16–32, 1 Samuel 9:1–10:16, Psalm 55
May 27 - Romans 2:1–3:8, 1 Samuel 10:17–11:15, Psalm 56
May 28 - Romans 3:9–31, 1 Samuel 12, Psalm 57
May 29 - Romans 4, 1 Samuel 13, Psalm 58
May 30 - Romans 5, 1 Samuel 14, Psalm 59
May 31 - Romans 6, 1 Samuel 15, Psalm 60

BIBLE READINGS FOR JUNE

June 1 - ROMANS 7, 1 SAMUEL 16, PSALM 61
June 2 - ROMANS 8 1 SAMUEL 17:1–54, PSALM 62
June 3 - ROMANS 9:1–29, 1 SAMUEL 17:55–18:30, PSALM 63
June 4 - ROMANS 9:30–10:21, 1 SAMUEL 19, PSALM 64
June 5 - ROMANS 11:1–24, 1 SAMUEL 20, PSALM 65
June 6 - ROMANS 11:25–36, 1 SAMUEL 21–22, PSALM 66
June 7 - ROMANS 12, 1 SAMUEL 23–24, PSALM 67
June 8 - ROMANS 13, 1 SAMUEL 25, PSALM 68
June 9 - ROMANS 14, 1 SAMUEL 26, PSALM 69
June 10 - ROMANS 15:1–13, 1 SAMUEL 27–28, PSALM 70
June 11 - ROMANS 15:14–33, 1 SAMUEL 29–31, PSALM 71
June 12 - ROMANS 16, 2 SAMUEL 1, PSALM 72
June 13 - MARK 1:1–20, 2 SAMUEL 2:1–3:1, DANIEL 1
June 14 - MARK 1:21–45, 2 SAMUEL 3:2–39, DANIEL 2:1–23
June 15 - MARK 2, 2 SAMUEL 4–5, DANIEL 2:24–49
June 16 - MARK 3:1–19, 2 SAMUEL 6, DANIEL 3
June 17 - MARK 3:20–35, 2 SAMUEL 7–8, DANIEL 4
June 18 - MARK 4:1–20, 2 SAMUEL 9–10, DANIEL 5
June 19 - MARK 4:21–41, 2 SAMUEL 11–12, DANIEL 6
June 20 - MARK 5:1–20, 2 SAMUEL 13, DANIEL 7
June 21 - MARK 5:21–43, 2 SAMUEL 14, DANIEL 8
June 22 - MARK 6:1–29, 2 SAMUEL 15, DANIEL 9
June 23 - MARK 6:30–56, 2 SAMUEL 16, DANIEL 10
June 24 - MARK 7:1–13, 2 SAMUEL 17, DANIEL 11:1–19
June 25 - MARK 7:14–37, 2 SAMUEL 18, DANIEL 11:20–45
June 26 - MARK 8:1–21, 2 SAMUEL 19, DANIEL 12
June 27 - MARK 8:22–9:1, 2 SAMUEL 20–21, HOSEA 1:1–2:1
June 28 - MARK 9:2–50, 2 SAMUEL 22, HOSEA 2:2–23
June 29 - MARK 10:1–31, 2 SAMUEL 23, HOSEA 3
June 30 - MARK 10:32–52, 2 SAMUEL 24, HOSEA 4:1–11

BIBLE READINGS FOR JULY

July 1 - MARK 11:1–14, 1 KINGS 1, HOSEA 4:12–5:4
July 2 - MARK 11:15–33, 1 KINGS 2, HOSEA 5:5–15
July 3 - MARK 12:1–27, 1 KINGS 3, HOSEA 6:1–7:2
July 4 - MARK 12:28–44, 1 KINGS 4-5, HOSEA 7:3–16
July 5 - MARK 13:1–13, 1 KINGS 6, HOSEA 8
July 6 - MARK 13:14–37, 1 KINGS 7, HOSEA 9:1–16
July 7 - MARK 14:1–31, 1 KINGS 8, HOSEA 9:17–10:15
July 8 - MARK 14:32–72, 1 KINGS 9, HOSEA 11:1–11
July 9 - MARK 15:1–20, 1 KINGS 10, HOSEA 11:12–12:14
July 10 - MARK 15:21–47, 1 KINGS 11, HOSEA 13
July 11 - MARK 16, 1 KINGS 12:1–31, HOSEA 14
July 12 - 1 CORINTHIANS 1:1–17, 1 KINGS 12:32–13:34, JOEL 1
July 13 - 1 CORINTHIANS 1:18–31, 1 KINGS 14, JOEL 2:1–11
July 14 - 1 CORINTHIANS 2, 1 KINGS 15:1–32, JOEL 2:12–32
July 15 - 1 CORINTHIANS 3, 1 KINGS 15:33–16:34, JOEL 3
July 16 - 1 CORINTHIANS 4, 1 KINGS 17, AMOS 1
July 17 - 1 CORINTHIANS 5, 1 KINGS 18, AMOS 2:1–3:2
July 18 - 1 CORINTHIANS 6, 1 KINGS 19, AMOS 3:3–4:3
July 19 - 1 CORINTHIANS 7:1–24, 1 KINGS 20, AMOS 4:4–13
July 20 - 1 CORINTHIANS 7:25–40, 1 KINGS 21, AMOS 5
July 21 - 1 CORINTHIANS 8, 1 KINGS 22, AMOS 6
July 22 - 1 CORINTHIANS 9, 2 KINGS 1–2, AMOS 7
July 23 - 1 CORINTHIANS 10, 2 KINGS 3, AMOS 8
July 24 - 1 CORINTHIANS 11:1–16, 2 KINGS 4, AMOS 9
July 25 - 1 CORINTHIANS 11:17–34, 2 KINGS 5, OBADIAH
July 26 - 1 CORINTHIANS 12, 2 KINGS 6:1–7:2, JONAH 1
July 27 - 1 CORINTHIANS 13, 2 KINGS 7:3–20, JONAH 2
July 28 - 1 CORINTHIANS 14:1–25, 2 KINGS 8, JONAH 3
July 29 - 1 CORINTHIANS 14:26–40, 2 KINGS 9, JONAH 4
July 30 - 1 CORINTHIANS 15:1–34, 2 KINGS 10, MICAH 1
July 31 - 1 CORINTHIANS 15:35–58, 2 KINGS 11, MICAH 2

BIBLE READINGS FOR AUGUST

August 1 - 1 CORINTHIANS 16, 2 KINGS 12–13, MICAH 3
August 2 - 2 CORINTHIANS 1:1–2:4, 2 KINGS 14, MICAH 4:1–5:1
August 3 - 2 CORINTHIANS 2:5–3:18, 2 KINGS 15–16, MICAH 5:2–15
August 4 - 2 CORINTHIANS 4:1–5:10, 2 KINGS 17, MICAH 6
August 5 - 2 CORINTHIANS 5:11–6:13, 2 KINGS 18, MICAH 7
August 6 - 2 CORINTHIANS 6:14–7:16, 2 KINGS 19, NAHUM 1
August 7 - 2 CORINTHIANS 8, 2 KINGS 20–21, NAHUM 2
August 8 - 2 CORINTHIANS 9, 2 KINGS 22:1–23:35, NAHUM 3
August 9 - 2 CORINTHIANS 10, 2 KINGS 23:36–24:20, HABAKKUK 1
August 10 - 2 CORINTHIANS 11, 2 KINGS 25, HABAKKUK 2
August 11 - 2 CORINTHIANS 12, 1 CHRONICLES 1–2, HABAKKUK 3
August 12 - 2 CORINTHIANS 13, 1 CHRONICLES 3–4, ZEPHANIAH 1
August 13 - JOHN 1:1–18, 1 CHRONICLES 5–6, ZEPHANIAH 2
August 14 - JOHN 1:19–34, 1 CHRONICLES 7–8, ZEPHANIAH 3
August 15 - JOHN 1:35–51, 1 CHRONICLES 9, HAGGAI 1–2
August 16 - JOHN 2, 1 CHRONICLES 10–11, ZECHARIAH 1
August 17 - JOHN 3:1–21, 1 CHRONICLES 12, ZECHARIAH 2
August 18 - JOHN 3:22–36, 1 CHRONICLES 13–14, ZECHARIAH 3
August 19 - JOHN 4:1–26, 1 CHRONICLES 15:1–16:6, ZECHARIAH 4
August 20 - JOHN 4:27–42, 1 CHRONICLES 16:7–43, ZECHARIAH 5
August 21 - JOHN 4:43–54, 1 CHRONICLES 17, ZECHARIAH 6
August 22 - JOHN 5:1–18, 1 CHRONICLES 18–19, ZECHARIAH 7
August 23 - JOHN 5:19–47, 1 CHRONICLES 20:1–22:1, ZECHARIAH 8
August 24 - JOHN 6:1–21, 1 CHRONICLES 22:2–23:32, ZECHARIAH 9
August 25 - JOHN 6:22–59, 1 CHRONICLES 24, ZECHARIAH 10
August 26 - JOHN 6:60–71, 1 CHRONICLES 25–26, ZECHARIAH 11
August 27 - JOHN 7:1–24, 1 CHRONICLES 27–28, ZECHARIAH 12
August 28 - JOHN 7:25–52, 1 CHRONICLES 29, ZECHARIAH 13
August 29 - JOHN 8:1–20, 2 CHRONICLES 1:1–2:16, ZECHARIAH 14
August 30 - JOHN 8:21–47, 2 CHRONICLES 2:17–5:1, MALACHI 1:1–2:9
August 31 - JOHN 8:48–59, 2 CHRONICLES 5:2–14, MALACHI 2:10–16

BIBLE READINGS FOR SEPTEMBER

September 1 - JOHN 9:1–23, 2 CHRONICLES 6, MALACHI 2:17–3:18
September 2 - JOHN 9:24–41, 2 CHRONICLES 7, MALACHI 4
September 3 - JOHN 10:1–21, 2 CHRONICLES 8, PSALM 73
September 4 - JOHN 10:22–42, 2 CHRONICLES 9, PSALM 74
September 5 - JOHN 11:1–27, 2 CHRONICLES 10–11, PSALM 75
September 6 - JOHN 11:28–57, 2 CHRONICLES 12–13, PSALM 76
September 7 - JOHN 12:1–26, 2 CHRONICLES 14–15, PSALM 77
September 8 - JOHN 12:27–50, 2 CHRONICLES 16–17, PSALM 78:1–20
September 9 - JOHN 13:1–20, 2 CHRONICLES 18, PSALM 78:21–37
September 10 - JOHN 13:21–38, 2 CHRONICLES 19, PSALM 78:38–55
September 11 - JOHN 14:1–14, 2 CHRONICLES 20:1–21:1, PSALM
      78:56–72
September 12 - JOHN 14:15–31, 2 CHRONICLES 21:2–22:12, PSALM 79
September 13 - JOHN 15:1–16:4, 2 CHRONICLES 23, PSALM 80
September 14 - JOHN 16:4–33, 2 CHRONICLES 24, PSALM 81
September 15 - JOHN 17, 2 CHRONICLES 25, PSALM 82
September 16 - JOHN 18:1–18, 2 CHRONICLES 26, PSALM 83
September 17 - JOHN 18:19–38, 2 CHRONICLES 27–28, PSALM 84
September 18 - JOHN 18:38–19:16, 2 CHRONICLES 29, PSALM 85
September 19 - JOHN 19:16–42, 2 CHRONICLES 30, PSALM 86
September 20 - JOHN 20:1–18, 2 CHRONICLES 31, PSALM 87
September 21 - JOHN 20:19–31, 2 CHRONICLES 32, PSALM 88
September 22 - JOHN 21, 2 CHRONICLES 33, PSALM 89:1–18
September 23 - 1 JOHN 1, 2 CHRONICLES 34, PSALM 89:19–37
September 24 - 1 JOHN 2, 2 CHRONICLES 35, PSALM 89:38–52
September 25 - 1 JOHN 3, 2 CHRONICLES 36, PSALM 90
September 26 - 1 JOHN 4, EZRA 1–2, PSALM 91
September 27 - 1 JOHN 5, EZRA 3–4, PSALM 92
September 28 - 2 JOHN, EZRA 5–6, PSALM 93
September 29 - 3 JOHN, EZRA 7–8, PSALM 94
September 30 - JUDE, EZRA 9–10, PSALM 95

Bible Readings for October

October 1 - REVELATION 1, NEHEMIAH 1–2, PSALM 96
October 2 - REVELATION 2, NEHEMIAH 3, PSALM 97
October 3 - REVELATION 3, NEHEMIAH 4, PSALM 98
October 4 - REVELATION 4, NEHEMIAH 5:1–7:4, PSALM 99
October 5 - REVELATION 5, NEHEMIAH 7:5–8:12, PSALM 100
October 6 - REVELATION 6, NEHEMIAH 8:13–9:37, PSALM 101
October 7 - REVELATION 7, NEHEMIAH 9:38–10:39, PSALM 102
October 8 - REVELATION 8, NEHEMIAH 11, PSALM 103
October 9 - REVELATION 9, NEHEMIAH 12, PSALM 104:1–23
October 10 - REVELATION 10, NEHEMIAH 13, PSALM 104:24–35
October 11 - REVELATION 11, ESTHER 1, PSALM 105:1–25
October 12 - REVELATION 12, ESTHER 2, PSALM 105:26–45
October 13 - REVELATION 13, ESTHER 3–4, PSALM 106:1–23
October 14 - REVELATION 14, ESTHER 5:1–6:13, PSALM 106:24–48
October 15 - REVELATION 15, ESTHER 6:14–8:17, PSALM 107:1–22
October 16 - REVELATION 16, ESTHER 9–10, PSALM 107:23–43
October 17 - REVELATION 17, ISAIAH 1–2, PSALM 108
October 18 - REVELATION 18, ISAIAH 3–4, PSALM 109:1–19
October 19 - REVELATION 19, ISAIAH 5–6, PSALM 109:20–31
October 20 - REVELATION 20, ISAIAH 7–8, PSALM 110
October 21 - REVELATION 21–22, ISAIAH 9–10, PSALM 111
October 22 - 1 THESSALONIANS 1, ISAIAH 11–13, PSALM 112
October 23 - 1 THESSALONIANS 2:1–16, ISAIAH 14–16, PSALM 113
October 24 - 1 THESSALONIANS 2:17–3:13, ISAIAH 17–19, PSALM 114
October 25 - 1 THESSALONIANS 4, ISAIAH 20–22, PSALM 115
October 26 - 1 THESSALONIANS 5, ISAIAH 23–24, PSALM 116
October 27 - 2 THESSALONIANS 1, ISAIAH 25–26, PSALM 117
October 28 - 2 THESSALONIANS 2, ISAIAH 27–28, PSALM 118
October 29 - 2 THESSALONIANS 3, ISAIAH 29–30, PSALM 119:1–32
October 30 - 1 TIMOTHY 1, ISAIAH 31–33, PSALM 119:33–64
October 31 - 1 TIMOTHY 2, ISAIAH 34–35, PSALM 119:65–96

Bible Readings for November

November 1 - 1 Timothy 3, Isaiah 36–37, Psalm 119:97–120
November 2 - 1 Timothy 4, Isaiah 38–39, Psalm 119:121–144
November 3 - 1 Timothy 5:1–22, Jeremiah 1–2, Psalm 119:145–176
November 4 - 1 Timothy 5:23–6:21, Jeremiah 3–4, Psalm 120
November 5 - 2 Timothy 1, Jeremiah 5–6, Psalm 121
November 6 - 2 Timothy 2, Jeremiah 7–8, Psalm 122
November 7 - 2 Timothy 3, Jeremiah 9–10, Psalm 123
November 8 - 2 Timothy 4, Jeremiah 11–12, Psalm 124
November 9 - Titus 1, Jeremiah 13–14, Psalm 125
November 10 - Titus 2, Jeremiah 15–16, Psalm 126
November 11 - Titus 3, Jeremiah 17–18, Psalm 127
November 12 - Philemon, Jeremiah 19–20, Psalm 128
November 13 - James 1, Jeremiah 21–22, Psalm 129
November 14 - James 2, Jeremiah 23–24, Psalm 130
November 15 - James 3, Jeremiah 25–26, Psalm 131
November 16 - James 4, Jeremiah 27–28, Psalm 132
November 17 - James 5, Jeremiah 29–30, Psalm 133
November 18 - 1 Peter 1, Jeremiah 31–32, Psalm 134
November 19 - 1 Peter 2, Jeremiah 33–34, Psalm 135
November 20 - 1 Peter 3, Jeremiah 35–36, Psalm 136
November 21 - 1 Peter 4, Jeremiah 37–38, Psalm 137
November 22 - 1 Peter 5, Jeremiah 39–40, Psalm 138
November 23 - 2 Peter 1, Jeremiah 41–42, Psalm 139
November 24 - 2 Peter 2, Jeremiah 43–44, Psalm 140
November 25 - 2 Peter 3, Jeremiah 45–46, Psalm 141
November 26 - Galatians 1, Jeremiah 47–48, Psalm 142
November 27 - Galatians 2, Jeremiah 49–50, Psalm 143
November 28 - Galatians 3:1–18, Jeremiah 51–52, Psalm 144
November 29 - Galatians 3:19–4:20, Lamentations 1–2, Psalm 145
November 30 - Galatians 4:21–31, Lamentations 3–4, Psalm 146

Bible Readings for December

December 1 - GALATIANS 5:1–15, LAMENTATIONS 5, PSALM 147
December 2 - GALATIANS 5:16–26, EZEKIEL 1, PSALM 148
December 3 - GALATIANS 6, EZEKIEL 2–3, PSALM 149
December 4 - EPHESIANS 1, EZEKIEL 4–5, PSALM 150
December 5 - EPHESIANS 2, EZEKIEL 6–7, ISAIAH 40
December 6 - EPHESIANS 3, EZEKIEL 8–9, ISAIAH 41
December 7 - EPHESIANS 4:1–16, EZEKIEL 10–11, ISAIAH 42
December 8 - EPHESIANS 4:17–32, EZEKIEL 12–13, ISAIAH 43
December 9 - EPHESIANS 5:1–20, EZEKIEL 14–15, ISAIAH 44
December 10 - EPHESIANS 5:21–33, EZEKIEL 16, ISAIAH 45
December 11 - EPHESIANS 6, EZEKIEL 17, ISAIAH 46
December 12 - PHILIPPIANS 1:1–11, EZEKIEL 18, ISAIAH 47
December 13 - PHILIPPIANS 1:12–30, EZEKIEL 19, ISAIAH 48
December 14 - PHILIPPIANS 2:1–11, EZEKIEL 20, ISAIAH 49
December 15 - PHILIPPIANS 2:12–30, EZEKIEL 21–22, ISAIAH 50
December 16 - PHILIPPIANS 3, EZEKIEL 23, ISAIAH 51
December 17 - PHILIPPIANS 4, EZEKIEL 24, ISAIAH 52
December 18 - COLOSSIANS 1:1–23, EZEKIEL 25–26, ISAIAH 53
December 19 - COLOSSIANS 1:24–2:19, EZEKIEL 27–28, ISAIAH 54
December 20 - COLOSSIANS 2:20–3:17, EZEKIEL 29–30, ISAIAH 55
December 21 - COLOSSIANS 3:18–4:18, EZEKIEL 31–32, ISAIAH 56
December 22 - LUKE 1:1–25, EZEKIEL 33, ISAIAH 57
December 23 - LUKE 1:26–56, EZEKIEL 34, ISAIAH 58
December 24 - LUKE 1:57–80, EZEKIEL 35–36, ISAIAH 59
December 25 - LUKE 2:1–20, EZEKIEL 37, ISAIAH 60
December 26 - LUKE 2:21–52, EZEKIEL 38–39, ISAIAH 61
December 27 - LUKE 3:1–20, EZEKIEL 40–41, ISAIAH 62
December 28 - LUKE 3:21–38, EZEKIEL 42–43, ISAIAH 63
December 29 - LUKE 4:1–30, EZEKIEL 44–45, ISAIAH 64
December 30 - LUKE 4:31–44, EZEKIEL 46–47, ISAIAH 65
December 31 - LUKE 5:1–26, EZEKIEL 48, ISAIAH 66